Transcend

Forrest Limon and Nathan Wagner

DEDICATION

Forrest

To my grandmother, Dr. Patricia O'Boyle; and my
loving parents Robert and Maureen Limon

Nathan

To my parents, Michael and Tammy Wagner; and my
brothers for nurturing these values so that I may
share them with you

CONTENTS

ACKNOWLEDGMENTS

We are eternally grateful for the following people for their shared time, wisdom, and support:

Coach Bill Hall, Dr. Susan Saylor, Kirby Pickle, and Sarah Cohen.

And to the following organizations:

J.P. Morgan Chase, Mercy College, Sherando Football, The Town of Middletown, and The Virginia Polytechnic Institute and State University.

Lastly, we want to thank God for giving us the ability and opportunity to take on such an endeavor.

I. INTRODUCTION

What is your purpose? Take a moment to think. Have you come up with anything yet? How specific or definite is your purpose? What motivates you? You may have an answer, you may not have any idea at all, or you may be somewhere in between. Whether you know it or not, everyone has a purpose. Likewise, many people have goals, wishes, and desires to fulfill. Some are very achievable, some achievable with a lot of work in the right direction, and others unrealistic without the right set of tools. The purpose of this short guide is to help you realize your potential and maximize it with relentless pursuit.

Becoming the best version of yourself is a beautiful struggle. You must find your definite purpose, but you must also find your balance. By these means, you can be constantly improving while keeping your sanity. After all, you're only really competing with yourself. What is realizing and maximizing potential?

In short, realizing your potential is a combination of confidence, empowerment, and awareness. Realizing your potential is the ability to understand how great you can be and that for the most part, you are in control. Every human has unlimited potential; the only restriction is time. If you are constantly becoming a better person in some aspect, then you are living your best life. Maximizing your potential is the actual action taken to efficiently improve. To maximize your potential is to close the gap between where you are today and where you want to be tomorrow. Remember this quote from Abraham Lincoln as you read forward, "The best way to predict the future is to create it." Take the following principles to heart and exercise them daily so you may have the proper tools to realize and maximize your individual potential.

Throughout this book, we will provide you with outside research and examples, together with personal insight in hopes to relate. Before inserting personal examples and thoughts, the section header will indicate the name of the author who is reflecting on a topic. Enjoy.

II. BE LIKE WATER

The human body is amazing. Bill Gates, co-founder of Microsoft Corp. and one of the globe's leading philanthropists said, "The human body is the most complex system ever created. The more we learn about it, the more appreciation we have about what a rich system it is." Despite the complexity of our body and its functionality, there is one stunning biological truth: up to 60% of the adult human body is made up of water, such a simple fuel. Water, the main constituent of our earth's streams, lakes, and oceans accounts for 71% of planet Earth. We can all agree that water is of extreme importance for our survival. As we analyze water and its unique characteristics a bit further, we will find its simplest traits can be implemented into our own lives to better realize and maximize our full potential. We only ask you to do a few things to realize your potential, the first...be transparent.

1. Be Transparent

It's half past midnight, and you are interrupted by the sudden thirst for water before being able to sleep further. You walk into the kitchen to pour a glass of water and then you return to your bed. This picture must be familiar. In this event, focus on the water being poured into your glass. What do you see? Simple yet powerful characteristics can be observed if you open your mind. Characteristic number one, transparency. Being transparent with yourself and others is extremely important to realizing your potential. Also, transparency leads to a more fulfilling and happier existence. You must be transparent with yourself, as it becomes easier to then be transparent with others.

President Thomas Jefferson wrote, "Honesty is the first chapter in the book of wisdom." Water is clear, just as you should be. Clarity and honesty are one and the same in this instance. Be honest with yourself. For us, that means looking in the mirror and reflecting on the occurrences of the day. It is important to recognize both positive and negative results from a day's work. Assess whether or not certain occurrences align with who you want to become. Look at yourself in the mirror with sound judgment and a growth mindset. The mirror tactic is helpful for assessment because it is a time of reflection. Honesty by definition is telling the truth or admitting to a lie. To be truly honest with yourself, it takes diving deep into the reason behind the act. Assess your day and ask yourself, "Where can I improve?" You are not perfect and can improve anything you do. It will be easy to criticize the lows of the day, but there is also room for improvement in the highs. For instance, if you win a contest, maybe you were already at an advantage over others. The only person you should really be competing with is yourself. Honesty will encourage you to keep working further. It takes time to realize the potential you possess, and this book will better guide you toward realization.

The most common lie addicts tell themselves is that they can stop whenever they choose. Yet, only 1 out of every 10 addicts follow through with quitting. The reasoning behind the failure of the unfortunate 90% is dishonesty. Likewise, people partake in bad habits and time wasters that lead to regret. Common examples include binge watching TV shows or movies, abuse of drugs or alcohol, and neglect of family members or friends. Recognizing these habits in your life and knowing they can be destructive is the first step in being transparent with yourself. Face your reality. Think about what specialty you have. If you have trouble reflecting on your own strengths, use a resource such as the *Clifton Strengthsfinder* test. The test highlights your strengths in a wide variety of different areas and provides techniques to build off of them. Better yet, ask your closest friends and family members; you may be surprised to hear what they think about you. Taking self-inventory is a great start in being honest with yourself, in doing so, you may realize your individual sooner than you thought. Typically, it is best to focus on improving your strengths than trying to fix your weaknesses. Never limit your capabilities but work on your strengths to give you a head start on your desired success.

1.1 Authenticity

A large part of being transparent is found in authenticity. Do not pretend to be something you are not. According to the National Society of Professional Engineers, it is unethical to "perform services outside of your area of competence." This includes avoiding deception through lying on your resume or assuming a role you have not earned. You will not succeed in an area unless you have been through the proper training that preparation requires. This applies to everyone through the Law of Authenticity. An everyday example of not being authentic is seen in relationship building. Being authentic and transparent with potential friends, co-workers, and significant others is extremely important for a healthy start and a long beneficial connection. At times, people will fake mutual interests to gain the affection or approval of another person. Deep down this person believes one thing, but outwardly portrays another. This is a major problem in today's society and doing this in order to build a relationship will only lead to future sabotage with one or both parties feeling resentment. Be yourself, and you will attract people similar and dissimilar to you.

Wagner

As a freshman engineering student at Virginia Tech, I had little competency in my field. All I had was a willingness to learn and develop myself every day. In my freshman year of college, I decided to search for an internship for the upcoming summer, something I was advised not to pursue but needed for my journey, or so I thought. I had very few successes during my first year of looking for gainful employment. The reason why is very simple. I was searching outside of my individual competency. I overshot by applying to top aerospace companies, when I should have focused on steppingstones. As an engineer, I needed to first earn experience and succeed in the classroom before I would be able to portray to an employer that I'm qualified.

I ended up attending four career fairs and interviewing multiple times in my first year. I interviewed with General Electric Aviation, the Department of Defense Missile Defense Agency, the National Air and Space Museum, and other academic--related interviews. During my General Electric behavioral interview, I noticed the project engineer who was asking the questions had a slip of paper in front of him. That paper included a whole section dedicated entirely to authenticity. Imagine that. An entire weighted portion of an interview for a technical company was whether or not the person was transparent throughout the interview. After countless attempts interviewing for a position, I learned to be authentic. Instead of trying to prove I was something better than I could show, I focused on improving myself. I turned the potential skills talked about into actual skills because I realized the importance of transparency. There will be no need for nerves going into your next interview or opportunity for self-promotion when you are well qualified for the position and can authentically show it. I succeeded in later interviews for a full academic-scholarship at

Virginia Tech and a position at the National Air and Space Museum, concluding my first year of school.

We discussed that focusing on strengths is more important than weaknesses; however, if the flaw is detrimental to success or holding you back considerably then you must terminate it. A prime example of a detrimental flaw would be close mindedness. Being transparent is keeping an open mind. As humans, we have one or two options moving through life, to discover what is true for ourselves or follow the footsteps of others.

The majority of people on this planet believe they are right, or they know the better answer or solution to a problem. This is natural, but it doesn't make it right. You will think you are on the right side of an argument because your side aligns with your beliefs which are only validated by your own thoughts. You should never assume you are the best person to make a decision, even if you think the decision is for your own best interest. Have an open mind and consider outside perspectives in your decision-making process. Those outside perspectives, the people around you, have strengths where you have weaknesses, or more relevant experience and knowledge.

Knowing when to hold back from making your own decisions and recognizing the thoughts of others to have better judgement is a big takeaway from this section. It is smart to weigh a number of options before making a decision, not discounting the thoughts that are not your own. However, weighing every single option is inefficient at times. Having an open mind, enough to simply listen to other opinions allows you take note of multiple ways of coming to a conclusion. Keep a pros and cons list, to formulate the best decision as you collect information. When shoe shopping, even if you have an exact pair in mind, it is logical to go into the store to look at multiple styles. Look at the whole selection, perform a cost benefit analysis, to cater to your specific needs.

Limon

My childhood in the Shenandoah Valley of Virginia was great, but my education was elsewhere. Upon the completion of high school, I packed my bags for New York City to study finance for the next two and a half years. Seeking discomfort and great opportunity, the concrete jungle was a phenomenal place to start. What I learned outside the classroom, in addition to classwork, proved to be of extreme value.

Transitioning from a place with a population of 1,300 to a city housing 8.5 million, gave me no choice but to become open minded. I did not lose perspective or sight of my strong values and moral compass as I submersed into the city life, but I was exposed to people from all around the world with different perspectives, values, and compasses. Dealing with such diverse human beings in the classroom and workplace proved to be challenging. But in those challenges, my learning spiked. Having an open mind accelerated the learning process.

1.2 Open Mindedness

The idea of having an open mind cannot be discussed without introducing the well-known "Allegory of the Cave" taught by the Greek Philosopher Plato. In summary, this allegory is about a group of people who have lived in the dark depths of a cave their whole life. This cave is everything they know, and it is home to them. One day, one of the people from the cave stumble across an opening to the real world. This person is shocked by the beauties and realities of the outside and thinks to share his discovery with others. The man returns to the cave and begins describing what he saw. The other cave dwellers see him as a manic and do not believe his crazy story. People often rely only on what they already know and are comfortable with. These people, comfortable where they were, missed out on the true vast beauties of life. They chose to neglect this new, scary information because they were close minded.

This allegory represents the struggles people face when they come across breakthroughs and how they are condemned by the public. If the people in the cave adopted an open mind and trusted the man to see for themselves, they too could live a life of happiness. We ask that you keep an open mind and also be wary of those who are closed-minded, so you do not fall victim to an ending proportional to that of the great Socrates who was murdered for sharing his wisdom. Depressingly, many people go through life never witnessing the light whether because of mere ignorance or purposeful reject for the greater things they were meant to achieve. When you are subject to a new idea go out and experience it for yourself before you pass judgement and close doors. Keep this anecdote in mind as you continue to realize and maximize the true potential inside of you.

1.2.1 Failure and Feedback

Having an open mind will make you more susceptible to feedback. Open mindedness automatically attracts discomfort. This is another big takeaway, putting yourself out there, knowing it might lead to failure so you can receive beneficial feedback. You will fail. And it is a good thing. Failure is not something to be feared, but to be embraced. Since failing is inevitable, fail the right way. Fail to succeed. Fail so that you may receive valuable feedback. You will fall, so why not fall in the right direction?

There is a lot of growth from failure if handled the right way. You should fail for reasons unforeseen, out of your control, or by bad circumstances. You should not fail due to lack of effort, bad habits, or leaving things up to chance. You should fail because something was overwhelmingly challenging even after every known effort was exhausted. If you fail the right way, you have still won many small battles but just came up short in the war. Every available stone should be turned over before failure incurs. Failing the right way is a choice. This method of failing is constructive because you did not give up. Failing the wrong way is accepting defeat before a deadline is met. Failing the right way is failing due to inexperience, which if reflected upon can turn into valuable experience. There is a reason you have been told your whole life that the greatest lessons are learned from failure, it is time to start listening. Here are the steps that lead to growth after failure:

Step 1: Aim High

-   Be fearless; put yourself in a challenging or uncomfortable situation

Step 2: Try and Try Again

-   Exhaust all possibilities, never give up, and let time decide when you have failed

Step 3: Fail

-   Temporarily, this feeling will not feel good, but it will fade. Frame failure as a building block

Step 4: Reflect

-   Did you work to the best of your ability? Were you dialed into the situation? Identify major mistakes or regrets along the way. Recognize new strategies unknown before

Step 5: Implement

-   Use this failure and your reflection to grow or gain experience. Implement new strategies for similar encounters in the future

Step 6: Repeat

- Repeating this process will result in higher achievement than staying in your comfort zone as long as you stay committed to a growth mindset

"A Ship in Harbor Is Safe, But that Is Not What Ships Are Built For"

- John A Stedd, American Author

Wagner

I have been a straight A student my entire life. Many think this feat is great, but what if I used this perfect record as an excuse not to challenge myself? I had a thought while I was creating my schedule for my second collegiate year that led me to disgust, "Wow, 19 credits are a lot, what if I cannot handle the workload this semester? This is all new material, maybe I should lighten my load so I can get all A's again." I felt rebuke toward this thought almost immediately. The grades are significant because they signal to employers you are a capable learner in your area of expertise; however, this instance revealed a non-ideal mindset. School should be about learning, not a symbol of prestige. I should not feel threatened by challenging myself. I should go in confident, but also prepared. I was challenged extensively in my first year of college. During these challenging times, I grew more in just one year than during most of my comfortable childhood.

Allow us to leave you with this thought. You can go ahead and stay tied up in your dock, growing barnacles, or you can set sail to face hardship on your journey to become what you could be. Seek challenge and embrace it.

Public speaking is a prime example of failing to receive feedback. Speaking in public is initially awkward and extremely frightening for most, but the more you do it and receive valuable guidance along the way, the better you will be at it. This doesn't sound like failure, but constant pursuit to be excellent at a craft.

Remember a time you were chewed out for a mistake? Maybe by your boss, co-worker, teacher, or parent. How did it feel? Bad I am sure. Unfortunately, most people associate this bad feeling and "negative" criticism as insulting or demeaning. They feel as though they are under attack and will want to save face. The natural instinct in these situations is to defend yourself and come up with excuses. Don't play the victim card, not here, not now. Detach yourself from the situation and swallow your pride. First, realize the person does not hate you and they are simply frustrated with the situation. And if that is not the case, and they do indeed hate you, their feedback is useless, they are not seeking your best interest. Second, remember the person giving you feedback is doing so because they want what is best for you. They have insight and experience you do not and want to shed their wisdom on you. Take this feedback and be grateful that they care enough to notice your mistakes and give effort to help you improve. When a mentor or peer goes out of their way to give you feedback, be sure to listen and reply. A good response would include thanking them for their insight and stating that you will use this moment as a lesson, using the steps addressed earlier on failure. After the conversation has ended, reflect on the situation with the motive to be constructive. Think about the situation, your role, the result, and the other person's response. Try to pick apart exactly what happened and why. All feedback matters, but not all feedback is worth paying attention to. Pay close attention to the right judgements and observations, made by those who speak to improve and educate. To determine the value of the feedback, simply ask yourself two questions:

1.) Does the person have your best interest at heart? (Constructive Feedback)

2.) Is the person skilled in the area of criticism? (Credible Feedback)

Look at yourself in the mirror, be honest. Open your mind, see the world and its inhabitants as a breadth of knowledge awaiting to be grasped. Know that everyone is wrong individually, but together we are right. Everyone has a piece of what is right, but they are missing the whole. Listen for new ideas and perspectives. Embrace discomfort. Fail. Accept feedback. Reflect. Be transparent.

2. Be Formless

Lee Jun-fan, known professionally as Bruce Lee, was a Hong-Kong and American actor, amongst other things. It was known that Lee was able to catch a grain of rice in mid-air with a pair of chopsticks. He was able to perform countless push-ups with a 125 lb. weight on his back, he only weighed 130 lbs. Bruce Lee was simply a freak of nature, but how? Lee revealed the key to his outlandish accomplishments back in 2000. He said, "You must be shapeless, formless, like water. Become like water my friend." We cannot agree more, this is indeed an essential step to realizing the unrealized, which is the potential buried deep within all of us.

2.1 Adaptability

Pour a cup of water. Watch as the water gushes out of its original container into the glass. The water violently splashes about as it attempts to adapt and become one with its environment. No matter what shape contains water, water is always able to become the perfect mold. Strive to be like water in the sense of this adaptation. For the most part, people act like cement. They are placed into an environment where they change very slowly to match their environment. They play it safe as they ooze to fill their container. The worst part is, when they are finally the perfect mold for their environment, they dry up and get stuck there forever just like cement. They become stuck in a routine and are unable to break out. Some are very happy and content here where they are comfortable, but those of you who seek constant growth and improvement must move on to master a new environment.

Be FLUID not VISCOUS. The definition of fluidity is the ability to move or flow freely. Fluids have no fixed shape allowing them to adapt to different environments very quickly. The definition of viscosity is having the qualities of a slow flowing, thick substance like molasses. Here are some traits you may recognize within yourself or need to work on:

Fluid/Water

- Curious
- Teachable
- Spontaneous
- Courageous
- Open-Minded

Viscous/Concrete

- Stubborn
- Easily Satisfied
- Negative
- Follow a strict routine
- Fearful

The overarching trait necessary to be formless is to be adaptable. To become better at adapting, throw yourself in new situations frequently and assess how you react to this new discomfort. Avoid being negative in new terrain, you may just find you have a natural talent for something you have never tried before. Learning to adapt is key. It is impossible to experience every new situation in the time we have in our lives, but it is possible to train yourself to be proficient at picking up on things quickly. Here are the steps to become adept in adaptation:

1.) Throw yourself in new situations frequently

2.) Compare this situation to other experiences in your life and apply this knowledge

3.) Listen to your mentors

4.) Learn from trial and error

5.) Stay positive

6.) Continue to brainstorm for answers

7.) Keep failing until you succeed

Wagner

Previously, I mentioned my numerous attempts to gain a summer internship. Out of all my conversations with companies about their core values and ideal behavioral traits, I discovered one trait was more valuable than them all. Adaptability. Employers want to see you can handle new experiences well. They will not try to teach you unless they know you are teachable. Being adaptable is one of the most important traits to be successful in any situation. Adaptability is being able to learn on the fly. If you adapt easily, you can pick up anything and be skillful at it in a short amount of time. Learning techniques are key for academic and career success. Being exposed to a new situation, embracing discomfort, and adapting to the challenge in front of you creates an endless potential. This potential is in the ability to learn anything you set your mind on with relentless pursuit toward mastery. Let me lay out an example of a learning technique I adopted as a student. The Feynman Technique is best described in four simple, valuable steps:

1. Pick a topic you want to understand and start studying it. Write down everything you know about the topic on a notebook page. Add to the page every time you learn something new about it.

2. Pretend to teach your topic to a classroom. Make sure you're able to explain the topic in simple terms.

3. Go back to the books when you get stuck. The gaps in your knowledge should be obvious. Revisit problem areas until you can explain the topic fully.

4. Simplify and use analogies. Repeat the process while simplifying your language and connecting facts with analogies to help strengthen your understanding.

I have personally applied this technique in school, and it has become habitual. The results of using this technique enabled me to learn quicker and retain more for a longer period of time. Experiment with techniques such as this or other procedures to develop adaptability. Remember to not be concrete with these techniques and know it is okay to go out of order. Let things be fluid.

Friends share hobbies and interests; it's often the start of friendship. Unfortunately, friendships are torn apart by opposing pastimes and newly adopted leisure; this happens all the time! It's called The Schooling Effect. The Schooling Effect is what most young adults experience throughout middle and high school, though it is very evident in people's lives of all ages. The newly developed friendships can be positive or negative. It is important to stay formless and shapeless, especially when first entering unfamiliar ground with newly adopted friends.

For instance, you're out on a Friday night, at restaurant or bar, wherever. You meet a couple of strangers who you gain a liking for, and they seem like perfect friend material. You share the same love for drinking coffee, watching Netflix, or rooting for your favorite NBA team. Match made in heaven, right? No, well it's too early to tell. They might turn out to be friends that will last a lifetime; there is nothing better than spontaneous friendships. But for this example, let's proceed as follows: You later find out the same friends that shared those interests with you often partake in poor habits and have harmful motives behind their actions. They indulge their sorrows with instant gratification and choose to be motivated by greed. That's not a risk you want to take.

2.2 Risk Taking

The majority of people prefer shrugging off dysfunctionality for convenience. The dysfunction of poor actions and the convenience of having a social group. People who are less like water, formless, and more like cement, ooze and settle into what is comfortable. A big part of being formless is forming less. One advantage we have over water is the ability to shape into what we want to become; water, on the other hand, forms regardless. And while adapting to any situation you're in is key to moving through life, adapting to the wrong crowd or set of friends can be deadly to your journey. Tim Ferriss, author of Tools of Titans and The Four Hour Work Week preaches, "You are the average of the five people you most closely associate with." Be kind to all but selective of the people who influence you.

Limon

I have always been selective in who I surround myself with. Too selective at times, before learning to have an open mind, before realizing the extreme benefit of accepting all people to learn and also influence positively. However, I remain cautious in who I choose to spend the majority of my time with, only because I do believe we are the average of our closest colleagues. With weeks left before heading to New York City in 2017, I managed to schedule a meeting with Kirby "Buddy" Pickle, multi-millionaire entrepreneur and former CEO of the Dental Holdings Corporation and many others.

Entrepreneurship had interested me for a long time as both my father and mother have taken on entrepreneurship at key times in their lives. I didn't hesitate to ask Mr. Pickle what the keys were to be a successful entrepreneur. Mr. Pickle replied with, "Entrepreneurship is like surfing."

Mr. Pickle made a connection between entrepreneurship and surfing that relates directly to life and being formless in your endeavors. This metaphor has stuck with me ever since. These are the steps laid out by Mr. Pickle for a successful journey as an entrepreneur:

<u>Step One:</u> Getting Your Surfboard
- 4+ Years of Education, Fundamental Skills

<u>Step Two:</u> Paddling Out on Your Surfboard
- The heavy lifting and grit of working your way up

<u>Step Three:</u> Choosing and Riding Your Wave
- Locating an opportunity and pulling the trigger

These three steps are great, but Mr. Pickle was sure to mention that only following these three alone will lead to failure as a company owner. Never attach to the initial wave as the first will almost never bring one in to shore.

The executives, entrepreneurs, and the transparent individuals who are willing to adapt and be formless know when to catch a new wave before the old wave crashes. Jeff Bezos, founder and CEO of Amazon.com, Inc. also the richest man in modern history, knew that surfing on the wave of selling books would lead to a slow drift, lost at sea. Bezos saw an opportunity, a new wave of opportunity for Amazon, all-inclusive eCommerce. Its entrance into this online sector of retail has allowed the company to thrive, taking up almost 50% of all retail spend in the country. The company, as of July 2019, had dollar value greater than 998 billion dollars, making it one of the largest companies by market capitalization in the United States.

Time and time again, we see those who can adapt to change, and flow freely achieve excellence with consistency. Bruce Lee and Jeff Bezos were not superhuman by any means but masters of adaptation. Have shape in your personality and principles but do not become concrete. Form less when you are surrounded by negative externalities but challenge your beliefs and values as necessary. Hold true and fall back on your beliefs during hard times and do not allow negative pressures to damage your values. Being able to learn quickly in a variety of situations will unlock your potential in numerous ways. Hiring managers of large-scale companies and millionaire entrepreneurs agree that being adaptable is both desirable and beneficial for the individual and their eventual team or company. Make discomfort comfortable. Assure yourself that this discomfort is just a catalyst for growth, allowing you to adapt better.

3. Be a Universal Solvent

A solvent is a trait which allows one substance to dissolve another. For our purposes, a solvent is a person who can dissolve a problem. Water is commonly labeled the universal solvent because it is capable of dissolving almost any type of substance. To take after water is to be capable of solving a wide variety of problems. Here's the kicker. Not only is water able to dissolve its obstacles, but it does so almost instantly. As soon as water makes contact with a chemical, it begins to absorb and reduce it immediately. To be like water, you must begin to solve your problems as soon as they appear.

3.1 Problem Solving

Problem-solving is an extremely important skill. You do not have to be in an analytical field to value this skill. Being able to problem solve properly will propel you forward on your path to excellence by avoiding and eliminating delays. Remain aware of the key components of a project, goal or relationship. Recognize factors that may result in failure and fool-proof them. To be a great problem solver, you must be observant and have great situational awareness. Do NOT overthink and create problems that are not really there. DO be on the passive offense and recognize threats. Being observant allows you to be proactive in your problem-solving. Observation skills include speaking less to listen more, looking in on events and situations from an outside perspective, and scanning your environment.

A mindset of Proactivity over Reactivity is very significant. Significant in the manner that a problem can be completely avoided simply because you are paying attention. A reactive person is a subject of their environment whereas a proactive person controls their environment and thus the result. Being proactive will prevent the problem from occurring entirely at best or will allow you to kill the problem in its early stages at worst. Essentially, those who are reactive give up their own freedom to think, act, and decide for themselves. Unlike a reactive person, a formless person uses their surroundings to their own advantage whereas the former is beaten down due to loss of control. Being reactive will put you in a situation when you are no longer free to choose. You must act in response to the problem at hand, unknowing how it will affect the future. President Abraham Lincoln believed, "The best way to predict the future is to create it." Be proactive. Be in control of your future, so that you are not simply a product of the bad circumstances you are thrown in. Do not leave your future up to chance. Play with the cards you are dealt, observe, and eliminate your problems to live a fuller life.

Another important skill is confidence in your ability to solve the problem. You must realize your capability to conquer an obstacle before you can. You have the potential to solve, or at least learn to solve, any problem. Prime your mind with a can-do attitude before you attempt to solve a problem, and it will open your mind to many more possibilities to exhaust. Confidence is not pulled out of thin air, yet it is built through repetition. If you do not receive proper praise or other self-esteem boosters from your environment, be that source in your own life. Be self-motivated and have self-assurance. Humans are not meant to be concrete. Be confident that you can grow in any area, whether it is a strength or a weakness, and you will look at your problems with the right lens.

Here are the steps for good problem-solving technique:

1. Identify the problem

2. Brainstorm solutions immediately

3. Act toward solving the problem

4. Adjust the solution until the problem is eliminated

5. Make appropriate changes to ensure the problem does not return

3.2 Quality of Problems

We just touched on eliminating your problems, thus reducing the quantity. But what does it mean to change the quality of your problems?

Norman Vincent Peale was an American minister and author known for his work in popularizing the concept of positive thinking in the early 1950s. We want to highlight a conversation held between Norman Vincent Peale and Gene Tunney, the roaring 20s, heavyweight boxing world champion. Mid-conversation, out of curiosity, Peale asked Tunney how he achieved such great muscle strength and size. Tunney explained, "Every day, I push against enormous amounts of resistance, and by pushing against that weight, my muscles expand by demand." Peale being the thinker he was, thought. He thought for a long time about what Tunney told him, "expand by demand." He came to a realization: problems are similar to weights in the gym, problems are needed to get stronger. As more is demanded, more is expanded, for the better. A higher power, perhaps God, gives each of us problems. Problems are the resistance we must push against to sculpt our souls. If we didn't have problems, we wouldn't have life. Instead of asking for a better quality of life, ask for a better quality of problems. How you deal with these problems will determine the quality of life you have.

Wagner

My experience with having good quality problems is extensive for I am young and ambitious. At times, this ambition puts me in a scheduling bind. In my second year of college, I had the opportunity to be a peer educator for the honors college to teach a reading seminar and a mentor for an engineering living-learning community. Through my involvement in these two groups, a problem surfaced. The training for the mentorship and peer education were on the same day, at conflicting times, and were both deemed mandatory. I addressed the problem immediately by emailing the authority of each organization. By the next day, this problem was erased with very little time to worry. The honors college was very considerate and allowed me to miss a portion of their workshop for my mentor training. This problem was quality. The problem did not occur by mistake but was out of my control. The problem only occurred because I was very involved in both of these communities and was granted the opportunity for a leadership role. How could I complain about such a circumstance? These are the types of problems you want to have the opportunity to solve.

Better quality of problems is the result of actively solving your problems. This is much more achievable when there is a deeper meaning pushing you. Tapping into your passion is very important and will be mentioned in a later chapter. Remember you are capable of dissolving any problem. Also, begin the dissolving process as soon as a problem is recognized rather than tolerating or ignoring it. Lastly, know that quality problems are just opportunities to grow and jump-start your path to excellence.

4. Be Cohesive and Adhesive

Water has two very special properties which allow it to attract like and unlike molecules. Cohesion is the ability to attract like molecules, or individuals in our case. Adhesion is the ability to attract unlike molecules. Water is able to attract like molecules through hydrogen bonding, and it is able to attract unlike molecules in an especially strong manner if they are positive or negative. Be like water to exercise cohesion and adhesion so that you can attract the right kind of people on your journey.

4.1 The Power of Cohesion

Attracting like-minded individuals is important in becoming excellent. No matter your beliefs, it is important to have people in your life who agree with and support you. These people often appear in the form of family, friends, or co-workers. These people do not challenge but support your values. They help you build on your strengths and increase your productivity when you work as a team. There is power in numbers, and cohesion allows people of the same beliefs to come together to build or sometimes destroy. Having like-minded individuals will fuel your cause and build confidence, yet this type of relationship is not the only connection you should make.

4.2 The Power of Adhesion

A more difficult connection to make is one with different people. People who disagree and challenge your values. There is growth in challenging your beliefs, and these people may have a positive influence on you. With an open mind, you can be receptive to these perspectives and see how they may actually improve you. You may not share similar interests or methods to achieve a goal, but sometimes you still have a common goal. Diversity is important because people think differently. Different thoughts mean there are more options to exhaust when pursuing the solution of problems. These problems are bigger than the individual.

Hopefully, you have close friends or acquaintances who are dissimilar to you and challenge you to grow. The key concern with adhesion is that you have to realize what change is good or bad. There are positive people in your life that can have a positive impact if you let them challenge your beliefs, but there are also negative people who have skewed perception and malicious intent. We trust you know right from wrong and can determine if people are looking out for your best interest and the general population's. This challenging of beliefs refers back to keeping an open mind toward feedback. Unlike minds are the ones who keep you in check so that you do not sway too far one way or another.

One flap of a butterfly's wing can cause a tornado halfway around the globe. How is this possible? Our intention is to note that one small drop in the ocean can then create a tidal wave of events. Our lives are unpredictable, but predictability in that life is determined by the decisions we make. It is difficult to believe in the "everything happens for a reason" concept. There is so much free will. For this reason, it is safe to say that many things merely happen by accident but others by cause and effect. We like to believe things are out of our control; meaningful relationships and life-changing opportunities, are granted by God. This way, when the world throws fear, anxiety, and anger in between opportunity, we are able to manage that negativity by the sole fact that God was a controlling factor. But it is equally important to realize we have a lot of control over what happens in our lives and should not blame external factors.

The Universal Law of Attraction states that whatever we choose to give our attention to, whether wanted or unwanted, we will attract. There are many schools of thought on this one law alone. Our school of thought: the people you attract are drawn to you because of your actions and decisions.

This is not an accident. The Law of Attraction is two-fold; it works with two singular focuses that depend on each other: free will and a higher power. Having an everything happens for a reason attitude can appear reactive and automatically puts you in the position to reap the reward of nature. Nature acts in accordance with your moves in life. Cause and effect coincide with this law. You choose your actions and decisions, which can attract certain people. But the reason why you choose what you do and why people come into your life is natures doing.

4.3 A Touch of Diplomacy

Cohesion and adhesion are best achieved through proper communication practices. While the Law of Attraction will bring these people into your life, these tips will help to keep them and build healthy relationships. A great resource regarding diplomacy and communication is *How to Win Friends and Influence People,* by Dale Carnegie. We will present the most important principles, from this book, for interacting with people below:

1. Listen

    a. Process what they say to not only respond but to understand

2. Do not criticize

    b. Instead of commenting every time something goes wrong, give them sincere praise when they do right

3. Serve others first

    c. Give and sow before you expect to receive and reap benefit

II. Be Like Water

1. Be Transparent
    1.1 Authenticity
    1.2 Open Mindedness
        1.2.1 Failure and Feedback
2. Be Formless
    2.1 Adaptability
    2.2 Risk Taking
3. Be a Universal Solvent
    3.1 Problem Solving
    3.2 Quality of Problems
4. Be Cohesive and Adhesive
    4.1 Power of Cohesion
    4.2 Power of Adhesion
    4.3 A Touch of Diplomacy

III. QUOTING SHAKESPEARE

"There is nothing either good or bad but thinking makes it so."

-    William Shakespeare, *Hamlet*

1. Positive Mindset

Events are objective and have no bias. A person is the force that applies a positive or negative context to an event. Thinking about an occurrence is what gives it meaning, but whether that meaning is good or bad lies in the eyes of the beholder. Humans are emotional creatures who have instincts and initial reactions to events. In the case that these emotions push you toward negativity, attempt to subdue these thoughts. You are in control of what you think, so choose positive thoughts. When an event appears instinctually negative to you, try to look for subtle positives. Most people believe that getting fired from a job is a negative event. You can view it as such and pity yourself, or you can see it as an opportunity. Maybe an opportunity to get away from a dead-end job and take a chance on your dream job? Where one door closes, another one opens. Negative events that are out of your control often happen for a reason. They create the opportunity for growth as long as you prime your mind with positivity. You cannot always control the event, but you can always control your response, thus creating the outcome. A simple equation coined by Jack Caldwell in *The Success Principles* is:

$$Event + Response = Outcome$$

When you come across an event that is not how you anticipated, respond with persistence to have a positive impact on the result. In a sports game, there are always plays that go against your team's benefit. You can dwell on these plays, or you can respond by focusing on the next play to change the outcome of the game. Searching for opportunities in the now while dismissing the past is one form of positivity.

Positivity can come in many forms such as joy, trust, and love. It is a trait that everyone appreciates, and the effects of positivity on you and others is very significant. You are able to spread joy through smiling more and having a good balance of serious and humorous attitudes. People often ask others, "Why are you smiling?" The opposite should be asked, "Why aren't you smiling?" Everyone is blessed to be alive, and there are so many additional blessings in their lives. There is benefit in enjoying the little things in life, such as eating a nice full breakfast, sharing a laugh with a friend, or cheering at an exciting event. These are all things to be grateful for, and you should express this gratitude through your words and actions. One of the strongest actions you can take is smiling. But you don't have to wait to feel joy or gratitude to smile; a smile can be a source of positivity, not just the response to something positive! In times of hardship, people look toward leaders. If they see someone smiling, a leader smiling amidst a struggle, they will feel the energy and smile too. Smiling is so easy, and research shows it can completely change your mental health. According to a variety of surveys by Penn State University, smiling makes you look good, feel good and causes others to smile. Spread joy one smile at a time.

Another way to spread joy is to exhibit a balance of humor with your seriousness. Being serious, focused, and dialed in is important. Being serious all the time can be seen as negative; you must find a balance. Find humor in daily tasks; there is nothing wrong with jokes and having a good laugh, as long as that does not eliminate productivity. Humor and laughter are just as significant as smiling and will release chemicals in your brain to make you feel joy. Humor should always be through good, healthy intent. By this, we mean you should not be making jokes at the expense of another's reputation or even your own. It is never worth a laugh to degrade another's character or diminish their confidence, nor your own.

You can spread positivity in more ways than simply outwardly expressing joy. The next outlet for optimism is through trust. Trust is a firm belief of reliability in someone. By showing that you trust someone, you are spreading positive energy. Trust encourages people to achieve because they know they are being counted on to succeed. When you instill your trust in someone, they gain confidence. Trust is a method of positivity that will allow you to avoid worry in any relationship and encourage the other party.

1.1 Law of Radiation

Eric Kim, a research fellow in the Department of Social and Behavioral Sciences at Harvard University, conducted a long-running study tracking women's health. They looked at 70,000 participants' levels of optimism. The most optimistic women had a nearly 30 percent lower risk of dying from diseases such as heart disease, respiratory disease, and cancer. There have been numerous cancer survivors that attest that their recovery was dependent on a positive outlook and a will to survive. May your cup always be half full, never half empty.

Especially when you are around other people, always have your glass half full. When you are surrounded by negative people, do you ever feel that their energy rubs off on you as well? More often than not, negativity radiates and is absorbed by those around them. This is also known as the Law of Radiation. The same is true for positivity. What one outwardly expresses is bound to be reflected back to them; it works just the same as a smile! There's no question why positivity is one of the most attractive traits, alongside authenticity, for talent acquisition. No one wants to work alongside an "energy vampire." An energy vampire is a person who will drain you of energy. They will "suck the life out of you and your goals and vision if you let them."

Energy vampire is a term coined in the book, *The Energy Bus*, written by author and motivational speaker, Jon Gordon. There are ten rules to eliminate negativity and living a positive life, outlined in The Energy Bus. One rule, in particular, focuses on loving the passengers of your own bus. You are the driver of your own bus; you have the wheel, but that doesn't mean you can't invite people on your bus to share your enthusiasm for the road ahead. The more people you invite into your circle of positivity, the more positive energy that is created. The Law of Radiation only becomes stronger when more energy is applied.

1.2 Purest Form

Love is the answer to really tap into the power of positivity. This form of positivity exceeds others, as everyone is craving love. Rule #8 in Jon Gordon's book is loving your passengers. You have to share your enthusiasm with those around you but showing love for those same people will have an everlasting positive impact. Love is not always easy, but it is one of the strongest and purest forms of energy in existence. We are not asking you to show romantic love; this is very strong as well; we are asking you to show platonic love. Platonic in the sense that this love is inclusive, not exclusive. This love extends to all friends and co-workers and shows you have their best interest at heart and want to see them improve.

Here are five ways to love your passengers, inspired by Jon Gordon:

1. Give Them Your Time

2. Give Them Your Ears

3. Give Them Recognition

4. Serve and Expect Nothing in Return

5. Help Them Improve

We urge you to use this list of methods to cultivate a loving mind and soul. Never forget, self-love must be felt before you can expect to make others feel loved. Work on loving yourself first, and you will have an abundance of love to share. Love takes time; it is something to be nurtured, never neglected. Love appears in many forms and toward all ages. Showing love for an apprentice, a peer, or a mentor is different amongst these examples and takes another quality to be effective. This quality is maturity adaptation.

2. Mental Maturity

Maturity adaptation is the ability to fall or rise to the age of the person with whom you are interacting or the event in which you preside. The R in the equation $E+R=O$ does not just include responses emotionally, but also how you respond physically and mentally. Think back to adaptability; you must adapt to the situation to achieve the desired result. Take a networking event, for example. Depending on the event and the type of people you are dealing with, you must dress, talk, and act in a certain way (formal or informal). Doing so isn't being inauthentic; it is acting appropriately to your respective environment. The President of the United States is expected to wear a suit and tie when meeting with other world leaders; it's a sign of respect, and a presentation that I am sure is embraced by each individual who takes the role as President. Maturity adaptation is won and lost though, not in appearance, but in communication.

Maturity adaptation allows you to converse with all age groups. Most teenagers seem unable to have adult conversations because they are stuck in their realm of age and interests. Similarly, some adults become overly professional and cannot bring out their inner child at heart. Mentally mature individuals are open-minded enough to explore themselves at all levels of age. Age is a system of numbers, a validation of existence. This system of numbers does not measure maturity in any way, shape, or form, nor does it have to confine one's dialogue within a set age group. "When you move toward mastery, your brain becomes radically altered by the years of practice and active experimentation" (Robert Greene, Art of Seduction, 2015). Maturity is dependent on experience, not age. There are many cases of people being less mature than their age denotes. These people may be fun to be around, but perhaps lack objectives in their life. Nonetheless people should have a youthful heart, and this way, passion can shine through an individual, but this energy will actually serve a purpose, rather than be considered play.

The more people you know of different ages and backgrounds, the more understanding you will have leading to a mature mentality. Everyone has a piece of the puzzle, your puzzle. Some pieces might be larger than others, but you cannot complete a puzzle with just one piece. Connect and learn from all ages. A common statement that teachers use in school is that they always learn something new from each year of students. Do not confuse age with experience or superiority. After all, the most prosperous man alive is not the oldest man alive.

Mental maturity which is developed from connecting with all kinds of people will give you better clarity. Your eyes have only witnessed what you have seen in your life. Your brain has only processed your memories and experiences in life. Connections and relationships with others widen this view so that you can use the perspective and experiences of others in your decision-making. Think of perspective as different windows of a building. You can only see what is in your room of the building, the thoughts in your head, and through your window, with your eyes. You've learned to have an open mind; therefore, take action on that learnt behavior and utilize other perspectives in your decision-making. This way, you will have good, sound judgment to pursue your passions and ambitions while avoiding deceit and other malicious tactics.

III. Quoting Shakespeare

1. Positive Mindset
   1.1 Law of Radiation
   1.2 Purest Form
2. Mental Maturity
2. Be Formless

$$E + R = O$$

IV. HEAD ON FIRE

You received the tools necessary for going on a permanent journey. Pack your bags and bring those tools with you. They have just been sharpened, and you will continue to sharpen them along the way. You are now a subject of radical honesty and transparency with yourself. You will know when you falter in these principles, and you will be positive through these faults and correct any problems. You are open-minded and ready to be uncomfortable and grow. You can face this discomfort and adapt accordingly. You are confident in your potential. You know that you can achieve excellence if you learn and grow every day. You are aware of your surroundings and have realized your limitless potential. Soon, you will embark on a journey; you will meet people who you now see in a new light and attract them to join in your relentless pursuit. You will have distractions along the way; you will struggle and face hardship. But you are ready, for you do not fear these obstacles; they fear you. Love yourself and your passengers on this amazing journey. The first step in this journey, now that your bags are packed, is to fuel up. Fuel in the form of pure passion, obsession, and love for what you want. As if your head were on fire. It's time to maximize your potential.

1. Fuel

The executives of successful retail giants such as Wal-Mart and Costco work closely with the top managers of individual stores internationally. They work with the managers to ensure that the corporate culture is stable, ethical standards are being met, and that the store is running efficiently. The manager of the store has a big impact, but we would argue that initially, the manager of inventory has a bigger responsibility. Take a clothing line, for example; it's starting from scratch and opens up a store in your hometown. The founder of the company and the current board believes they will be successful in this location. They have the product, different styles, and colors; however, one thing they are unclear about is the publics' initial reaction.

The vision is clear; the product is there; the executives have realized the potential of their company. But realizing, as we know, is only the first step. To turn their vision into reality, the current executives use an inventory manager to keep track of all in-store transactions and customer feedback throughout the first six months of being open. The inventory manager will pay close attention to the consumers' likes and interests, as well as the products' success rate relative to where those products are placed in the store. With this focus and determination on finding what works and what doesn't, the founder, executives, and inventory manager will be pleased to see that their potential was maximized. Before you can blink, the same hometown clothing store has maximized their profits and globalized with over twenty stores internationally.

Let's say your significant other or spouse's parents come over for dinner. This is the first time eating with them, and you'll be preparing the meal! What will you cook? First, you will want to know what they like to eat. Do they have any allergies? Do they handle spice well? What if they don't eat meat? This meal could go one of two ways, good or bad. The odds of the dinner going well can be significantly heightened by doing simple research before even starting. This is what you need to do! Just as the company did not move too quickly to expand their stores internationally, you must not begin your journey to maximization without first answering a few questions about yourself. The concept of self-inventory is an important concept to understand. And it is only the first of many concepts to harness and activate before tapping into your maximum potential.

1.1 Taking Inventory

In our separate but parallel journey to maximize our respective potential, we must first discover our identity and really understand ourselves. We must find meaning and a driving force or fuel within ourselves before we can pursue an end goal. The purpose of the following list of questions is to uncover one or more pre-existing interests, desires, or passions that you may already be subconsciously pursuing:

- What activities excite you?

- What current events draw your attention?

- Do you enjoy being around others?

- Is there a particular subject you thrive in?

- Is there a particular compliment you receive from friends, family, or coworkers?

- Is there a problem you've always wanted to solve?

After answering these questions, you may be in touch with some childhood dreams or aspirations. What happens when these dreams appear unrealistic or unachievable by nature? First understand what you want; secondly, those pursuits must be framed under two consequences, benefit and result. Do your interests and pursuits bring benefit and results to the world? There are four key factors that will determine whether or not your dream can become a reality. Below, we will discuss these factors and why they are so crucial.

What are you great at?

One true teller of what you are great at, which will eliminate both confidence and arrogance issues, is to look at common compliments you receive. The best way to describe this is with the words of Chicago Bears nine-time pro bowl running back, Walter Payton: "When you're good at something, you'll tell everyone. When you're great at something, they'll tell you." If you aren't being told you're great in an area, look at the responsibilities you're given. The responsibilities granted to you by others, specifically, those who seek your best interest and those that you trust, are a direct reflection of some of your greatest strengths.

What are the societal benefits?

Pursuits that serve others in some way, shape, or form, yield the greatest internal reward there is, happiness. How does this pursuit affect other people around you? Are there a lot of positive results, or is this a purely selfish desire? Stay away from bad motives.

Does the world need it?

Wants come and go, but needs stay forever. Is there a problem in the world that your dream will solve? Will there be lasting change and fulfillment of needs at any scale, small or large?

Is the need already fulfilled?

There must be a demand for what you are proposing. If someone has already pursued your dream to the full extent, and there is no void for you to fill or no improvements to make, then this goal will be less achievable.

As we have learned, order matters! We have given you many questions to ask and steps to execute, but this must be done in appropriate order. Before answering the second set of questions, the first set must be identified. The purpose of the first set is to identify an exciting passion or interest. The second set focuses on the more realistic or applicable side of a skill. The combination of these two sets of answers, both the passion and the realistic application, will create a perfect mixture just as fuel is a mixture of chemicals that will propel you forward.

You need to work on your passions, or you will never identify your purpose. The concept of finding one's true passion is usually in reference to a single purpose; however, passion and purpose are not one and the same. Passion is a strong and barely controllable emotion. Purpose is the reason for which something is created. People have more than one ultimate passion, and it is the collection of these passions that will lead you to fulfill your purpose. Moving away from purpose, as it will be touched on later, passion is the fuel inside you that will be the driving force for your journey when it's ignited.

Wagner

From my experience, many people shy away or turn off due to discomfort when discussing passions because the truth is, a lot of people are unsure. As a young college student, the conversations about where I wanted to go to college, what I was interested in, and what I wanted to major in are all too familiar.

Except for a select few, many of my close friends and peers feel pressured into decisions and are forced to decide when sometimes, that is not the best approach. According to the Department of Education, "About one-third of all undergraduate students change majors within their first three years of study." My college roommate and I chose our respective engineering majors based on the information we had available to us, but we could not be 100% certain. In order to heighten that certainty, we joined clubs, talked to upperclassmen and professors, and pursued internships. We collected as much information as we could through our own experiences and the experiences of those in similar situations. With this information, we were more capable of identifying our passion and could use this passion to fuel our vehicle.

A vehicle is the profession or career you choose to carry with you on your journey. We will discuss the idea of a vehicle in the following chapter. Getting back to the bigger picture, it is a difficult situation to be in when you have yet to discover your passions. As a sophomore at Virginia Tech, I taught a Self-Improvement and Motivation Seminar through the Honors College with one main goal: to encourage others to realize and maximize their potential through the exploration and application of various success principles. During the closing of our final class together, one of my students posed a great question. She asked, "If you were to write your own book on success, what words of wisdom, advice, or concept would you include that was not touched on in this class or emphasized enough?" Many of my students agreed that they wanted a book that would determine their passions for them and give them one definite answer to resolve the fear of choosing the wrong path. I responded to this eager want by saying, "No one in the entire universe can decide what you are passionate about, you must choose your journey."

Referring back to early chapters, it is extremely important to keep an open mind and follow your passions. Passions change over time with new information and experiences. You can reveal these passions through self-discovery just as you can uncover new trails on your journey. Through new experiences, you will uncover a new passion or reinforce your current pursuit. As stated in the reflection, your passion is 100% unique to you and you only. Cars use petroleum, trucks use diesel, and rockets use chemical propellant. Each person runs on their own unique fuel. Do not fear choosing the wrong direction because if you are in touch with your identity and are aware of both exciting and applicable passions, you will be propelled in the right directions in pursuit of fulfilling a hunger, your purpose, that passion provides.

We know the importance of taking self-inventory and actively searching and identifying your individual interests. We are also aware that these passions must fit into the framework of society and be realistic enough so that there is no wasted time in your pursuit of maximization. There is a caveat to this fuel that we describe as the first step in maximizing your potential. The vehicle must be refueled along the way! Always make time to reflect on your interests, as they are always changing. There is a statistic that 90% of teenagers had a passion involving sports, music, or the arts; however, only 3% of jobs were in those industries. When the same teenagers were quizzed ten years later their passions changed dramatically.

We encourage you to take calculated risks, not impulsive risks. Passions do evolve over time. Ask yourself again; what are you good at? If you love to play basketball and dream of playing professionally but only stand at five foot five inches, then you should know that there were only two players that stood at or below a height of five foot five inches in the entire history of the NBA! Pursuing this passion would be impulsive risk taking if you were to ignore your other passions and their better-suited applications, passions that have much lower risk. Your most exciting passion isn't always the most applicable. Life is too short, and you have a long road ahead. You don't want to make any unnecessary pitstops or run into failures that could be avoided with decision clarity and understanding the concept of a calculated risk. Taking the time to align the most exciting passions with applicable ones is the key for a healthy fuel. Reconnecting with your passions or discovering new passions that might make your ride more enjoyable will keep your tank full and your vehicle in motion.

1.2 Sturdy Motives

Motivation should come from the heart. With the proper motivation, progress toward a goal will not wear you out. You cannot get burnt out if your motives are stronger than the daily toil. In order to achieve great feats and overcome seemingly overbearing obstacles in your life, you must have sturdy motives. A sturdy motive draws on a positive desire or experience as opposed to a negative one such as vengeance. A sturdy motive is supported by love, not hate. A sturdy motive is consistent through the test of time, and one experience should not deter or erase this drive. A sturdy motive is an investment, not a means to obtain instant gratification or simple pleasures. Many people act off impulse as opposed to a well-identified motive. Over time, this impulse loses its power, and you will lose sight of the reason you began a project or goal. To give a concrete example of a poorly developed motive, we can look into anything relating to instant gratification, the seven deadly sins, or revenge.

If you can't recall the last time you were begging your parents for that cool toy on the store shelf, then try recalling the last time you saw a child literally bringing themselves to tears over a toy that their parents would not buy for them. From first glance, it seems that the toy means the world to the child, especially when you see tears streaming down their face. But the parents of the child are mature enough to know that by the time they are back in the car to go home, their son or daughter will have quieted or maybe even fallen asleep forgetting about this desire. We are all logical enough to know that there is no point crying over things that bring us short-term happiness, such as an article of clothing or a new toy. However, not everyone is as logical as you would think.

People today, adults, complain and even cry over not having the proper amount of cream and sugar in their coffee. What is the difference here between the child in the toy store and the adult crying over a coffee? Virtually, there is no difference! The parents of that child who cried in the store might have gone through with the purchase if the child cried a little bit longer. Maybe if the child hadn't given up so easily, just maybe, he or she would have gotten their toy. But that's the key! Any motivation that is short-lived and can be given up on easily is the wrong motive! Motivation again comes from the heart. It should be identified within the heart from a place of love and passion, not want and unrighteous desire.

As the world becomes more advanced and technology makes life easier, essentially, the healthy motivations, the ones that last, are lost in the madness. Furthermore, strong morals and values that encourage healthy motives are lost and tarnished by the society that thrives on instant gratification. Jeff Bezos, mentioned earlier in the book, exploited a nation of those who love instant gratification. With a tap of a button, Amazon, Inc., will deliver ten new toys to your doorstep in less than 48 hours! It is not necessarily your fault for not being clear on your motivations at this point in time, but it is surely your responsibility not only to comprehend the material we are presenting but to act on it too.

An example of harmful motives includes but is not limited to these seven deadly sins:

1. Lust - intense longing regarding sex

2. Gluttony - overindulgence to the point of waste

3. Greed - overbearing desire for materials

4. Sloth - habitual laziness

5. Wrath - uncontrollable anger or rage

6. Envy - resentment toward what another possesses that you do not

7. Pride - putting yourself above others, corrupt selfishness

These motives are harmful because they will influence your sound judgement and following through with actions backed by these sins will fill you with regret. These motives may also harm others in your path. To avoid these sins, continue to reflect in attempts to understand your motives before you begin to act on them. Exercise restraint until sturdy motives are laid down.

Another key factor in determining a sturdy motive is to understand who you are doing it for. Are you doing it to fulfill a selfish desire, add a line to your resume, or to simply feel accomplished? These are not sturdy motives. A sturdy motive is one where the person in the scenario has the interest of others in mind. They question what kind of impact their action will have on others and are mindful. They better themselves not to be prideful and brag about their accomplishments; they have a motive that supersedes the individual. Having a motive that sprouts from a "bigger than me" standpoint will keep you motivated, knowing that it is not just your future at stake.

Whether you are aware of them or not, you have countless impacts on the people around you, and it is very empowering to know how much you can benefit the people around you by bettering yourself the right way. Many can relate to this idea of doing something for a team through their family. Parents are extremely motivated by their children because they want them to have a great childhood and provide both their needs and wants. A person who is motivated by their family or a greater cause than themselves will outlast any individual doing it solely for personal gain. The stronger and sturdier the motivation, the longer you can overcome difficult obstacles.

In regard to instant gratification, this topic is the consistency of motivation. An inconsistent motive is revenge. Often, revenge causes more problems than it resolves. Justice is not served by meeting an evil act with an equally evil act. Fighting fire with fire just burns down more buildings. The instant gratification gained from the relief of hurting someone that wronged you instantly dissipates as vengeance is fulfilled. The avenger will remain empty even after committing the wrong that they were inappropriately motivated to do. Consistent motivation will remain even after the task is completed because consistent motivation favors the process over the result, and the benefits are endless. Now you have an idea of some of your passions and what it means to have sturdy, lasting motives. You have your fuel; now, you are ready to select the appropriate vehicle for your journey.

2. Vehicle

A vehicle is a mode of transportation that will take you from point A to point B. In this sense, your vehicle will be your profession or career that will take you from where you are to where you want to be. There are many variations of vehicles in the concrete sense. There are many different modes of transportation, whether cars, planes, or boats. Then, once you select a mode of transportation, there are different styles as well as types that use different fuel sources. There are many levels to this and many different ways to categorize them. For the sake of simplicity, refer to the next page:

Vehicle	**Fuel**
*Car	*Electric
*Car	*Gas
Plane	Electric
Boat	Diesel
*Scientist	*Solve Problems
*Scientist	Exploration
Business Owner	*Solve Problems
Healthcare Professional	Help others

There are countless combinations of "vehicles" in the sense of careers. You could be involved with business, health services, political science, design, history, and any other imaginable field of study. Beyond that, there are different passions and motivations between each respective person that motivates them to choose that exact vehicle. As seen in the table above, there are two examples where the car is the mode (marked by asterisks), but their respective fuels are different. In this instance, we can correlate this to the mode where becoming a scientist is the mode of transportation from where you are to where you want to be, but one is motivated by a desire to solve problems, and the other is motivated by a desire to explore the universe. In another scenario, two people may share a similar fuel just as an electric car and plane do—the business owner of a nonprofit aim to solve problems in their community just as a scientist does. Now we can see that a person's vehicle and fuel can vary or be similar in different levels. This table simplifies the idea without going too far into details such as the different brands of vehicles or specific job descriptions within each field. Your vehicle is the career path you choose to fulfill your passions and apply them to an end goal that will reap great benefit! That is an important point to clarify; you do not choose your passion based on your job. You choose your job based on your passion. Now that we have defined the vehicle concept, we can jump into choosing the right vehicle for you and the specifics of your mode of transportation that will better equip you to maximize your potential and enjoy the ride!

2.1 Choosing Your Vehicle

Picking the right vehicle is a stressful time for many. That time can take days, months, or year for some, and the stress will only follow. This stress is caused by both internal and external pressures. These internal pressures include making the perfect first decision, which is practically impossible, and the external pressures of family and friends. Take a second and realize that you do not have all the answers, nor does anyone expect you to. Before we go into the specifics of your vehicle or career path, let us focus on the big picture. The first and most important decision you should make is your field of interest using the passions we discussed earlier. What field will provide the most opportunities for you to capitalize on in regard to your interests and your unique skill set? Some young adults know their vehicle and are pursuing it right now; others do not. You may not know the exact make or model, but you are leaning in some direction. To identify this direction, refer back to the exercise on fuel where you were tasked to combine what you like with what you are good at. If this approach does not work for you, then you may be a multipotentialite. Multipotentiality is when a person has such a wide variety of interests that one career path cannot fulfill all their passions. Thus, one vehicle would be insufficient for all the respective fuels. These other fuels can simply be put to use in hobbies or side projects, but in some cases, individuals are so talented at two or more unrelated things that they are urged to pursue a path in all of them together or separately. Whatever approach you find channels your fuels best will be discovered by the fulfillment of these passions along the way.

You don't choose your passion based on your job; you choose your job based on your passion (fuel comes first).

Limon

My father works at our family-owned jewelry store and is an award-winning, self-branded entertainer. My beautiful mother is an interior designer, a great one at that! She used to own and operate a small art business. I admire my parents' entrepreneurial spirit.

Even more, I admire the love they share for what they do. My father would always say, "You never work a single day in your life when you love what you do." I made a promise to myself that whatever I chose to do in life, I would have a strong love for it. That not only applies to my occupation but to the activities I engage in and the people I surround myself with. My passion started to present itself from the strong words spoken by my parents, and the strong will they had for what they did.

Entering college, I chose to manipulate my schedule in a way which allowed me to work half of the week. A semester for me would include five, three-hour classes structured into Monday and Tuesday. This way, I was able to work for the rest of the week. This was one of the smartest decisions I made in my young life, and fortunately, my school allowed it. In my first year of school, with the power of networking, I was able to work at two Fortune 500 companies, within my area of interest, finance. This was perfect for resume building, but more importantly, it allowed me to look at all the vehicles at the dealership and not be immediately bound into one!

High school and college are two great ways to gather clues and insights about yourself and your vehicle. But do not be fooled; you do not have to go to school to be knowledgeable, seek the wisdom you wish to gain! The knowledge that school provided me and the experience the companies gave me outside of the classroom were a strong pairing. That strong pairing later became unstoppable when I added the determination to carry out the ideas and guidance presented in this book. And after all of this, I still view each move as a steppingstone; I am not done yet.

The reflection above is a great example of how to choose your vehicle(s) based on your passions which are discovered through experience. Your vehicle will carry you to different and very specific occupations and professions, especially in the industry. For example, people dream about solving problems and thus become engineers. The field of engineering is the vehicle, but then there are specifics beneath that. These specifics are temporary. At any job in the industry, you will likely start at an entry-level position and work your way up to a more leadership-based role. Once you have begun pursuing a passion through a vehicle, it is important to remember to be like water. Remain fluid in the workplace and do not become set in stone like concrete. Do not become comfortable where you are. Vehicles require maintenance just as your field of work does. Reassess and reflect as you gain new experiences and further explore passions. The odds are that you will not uncover a midlife crisis during this reflection, but there may be a fork in the road where you can decide to further your involvement in a very specific sense. Greek philosopher, Heraclitus taught a simple truth, "the only thing permanent is change." Accept this as fact, and you will never fall victim to becoming concrete in an ever-changing world. Have you ever walked on a really ugly sidewalk? When this concrete was first planned and laid out, it appeared perfect. As time wore on, the concrete began to crack, and weeds began to grow through it, damaging the concrete.

This instance occurs because the concrete was ideal for a fixed world, but that is not the case. The world we live in is dynamic, and the way to avoid cracking is not to become fixed. Change and grow alongside the world!

3. Roadmap

3.1. Goal Setting Techniques

An objective is a specific step which enables accomplishing things within one's vehicle or side project. You will set and achieve many goals in the span of your life. The first step is to identify this primary objective or chief aim. An objective is like a checkpoint or a pitstop. You will drive a specific distance and decide on a good stopping point. An objective should be clearly defined. This objective should be fueled by passion, have smaller incremental goals along the way, and a well-defined timeline. The mnemonic SMART (Specific, Measurable, Achievable, Relevant, and Timely) goals is a great way to set goals, but it is missing a small piece, the passion or motivation behind the goal. If you are not passionate about your goal, it will end in two ways: before it is achieved, or you will feel unfulfilled. Sometimes, the passion is found in the way you frame the goal. Some goals focus on wealth creation, but who is passionate about just that? Isn't it more about what you can do with that wealth? The goal should be to learn and create as much as you can so that you are more valuable and can make a greater difference. Once you make up your mind on what you want to achieve, then break it up into smaller goals. For example, if your vehicle of choice is to become a brain surgeon, you also know that you must first go to medical school. And in order to go to medical school, you will have to achieve high marks. What's the overarching goal here? To become a brain doctor. But we also know that excellent academic performance is required first, so the goal for today is simple; you must skip the movies with friends, stay home, and study. Completing small goals today lays the foundation for bigger goals tomorrow.

3.2. Direction

Direction is all about driving the right way to get to where you want to be. Sometimes, you will have to go out of your way, run into obstacles, and need a detour to get where you want but always be sure you are working in the right direction. The popular statement that success is not a straight line is true, but there is still a general upward trend to achieve your defined success. This trend is the direction you should always keep in mind. Working hard is important, but if you spend all your energy working hard at a fast food joint when your goal is to become a scientist, then a lot of that effort is going to waste. Working hard at relevant tasks that align with your goals will put you in the right direction. If you want to learn to connect with people, read books on emotional intelligence, and make one-on-one conversations a priority. If you want to understand how the world works and fundamental laws, study and experiment with Physics. The goal outline, as shown earlier, is a great way to set a direction for yourself.

3.3.   Focus & Vision

Focus is the ability to give your attention to the present so that things go the way you want them to. For example, when using your vehicle to reach a destination, you must focus so that you do not crash along your journey. When you focus, you pay attention to the small details that compound over time. Everything matters, some things more than others, but the details can determine the ultimate result. Football is a game of inches; life is a game of seconds. One second too soon or too late, and the result can swing for or against your expectation. Laser focus will allow you to enter a state where nothing else matters except what is in front of you. The ability to use this focus will allow you to maximize productivity in your work and maximize the countless rewards that present themselves throughout your journey.

Vision is the ability to look into the future. A talented or experienced driver will look out into the distance to recognize potential dangers, road closures, etc. The same should go for your life. Use vision to recognize problems so that you can avoid them with minimal effort before you put yourself in a tight situation. Utilize your vision for the future you want to create so that you can act in the present to close the gap between your fantasy and your reality. Envision the changes and goals that you want and start toward them.

3.4.   Habits

A habit is defined as an action or tendency that is settled and is hard to give up. The question is, what kind of habits should you create for yourself? The answer is quite simple. Your habits should allow you to do smaller or more repetitive tasks the right way every time such that you will close the gap between where you are and where you want to be. Habits take the decision out of the action. Researchers at Cornell University estimate that we make 35,000 conscious decisions a day. Each of these decisions has their respective consequences. Take a moment to reflect on some of your habits and whether they have a positive, negative, or neutral impact on your maximization. Mark Zuckerberg, co-founder, and CEO of Facebook owns many of the same shirts and wears them every day. He does this habitually to take the decision out of what to wear in a given day, and this saves him time. We are not proposing that you monopolize your wardrobe, there are many simple and creative ways to make decisions ahead of time so that you follow through as you want. Another example of this is seen in dieting. Though it takes some extra effort to prepare meals ahead of time, it will ensure that you are eating the right kind of foods that align with your health goals. Those who are dieting and use meal prep are able to stick to their plan because they take the decision out of their hands ahead of time, thus improving their eating habits. A great way to take decisions out of your week is a method we call Sunday Planning. Every Sunday, after reflecting on the successes and lessons from the past week, we look forward to schedule the upcoming week. What you do with your free time is what separates you from everyone else. To be the exception, you must capitalize on those "down hours." Many people create goals or resolutions like reading more or journaling. To actually be consistent with these goals, schedule them into your week so that later, you do not have to decide between bettering yourself and binge-watching television.

The Sunday Planning System

1. Reflect on the past week

    a. What did you do right?

    b. What could you have done better?

2. Plan the upcoming week

    a. What do you want to achieve this week?

    b. How are you going to achieve it?

        i. Schedule everything that you get to do and everything you want to do on top of that.

To give an example of this, we will use a student. A student has obvious responsibilities, such as going to class, club meetings, and homework. Keep a template schedule that has all of your specific routine responsibilities because they should remain the same week to week. Each Sunday, go through and create a copy of this template for the upcoming week, including new details, such as events, activities, family plans, and anything else that is a one-time thing for this week. Everything we have said so far is most likely close to what you already do to schedule your week, but here is what will make your week even better. Schedule in things without deadlines or specific dates like a goal to "read more." Make the decision to set aside the time, and it will be easier to fulfill that part of your schedule when it rolls around.

Unfortunately, scheduling and deciding to exercise the right habits will not be enough. You must have the willpower, especially when there are a million excuses not to do so. We wish we could say that you can plan a habit and automatically do the right thing every time. A garden will always need weeding just as you will always have to be disciplined and maintain the habits you expect of yourself. You only need one good reason to stick with it, and that reason is because you want to be the best version of yourself.

3.4.1.   Compound Effect

Remember earlier, when we presented two seemingly different goals, becoming a brain surgeon and skipping a night out at the movies to study? It is difficult to picture yourself sitting in your dream car, just as it takes effort to imagine yourself in your ideal occupation. It's even harder when your friends are out at the movies, and you're back home studying. But it's much easier to envision and take action when you understand the simple, yet powerful principle known as the Compound Effect. The Compound

Effect is the principle of reaping a massive reward for a series of small tasks that are aligned with your objective. The magic takes place in the small tasks! Although the results are massive, in the present moment, the small tasks feel insignificant. But without these significant small tasks, the results are nothing more than a fantasy.

The small goals you set for yourself that work in accordance with your objective must be done consistently over a lengthy period of time. Would you rather have a penny today doubled every day for a full month or a check in your name for $1 million given to you today? On Day 10, the penny has grown to $5.12, and the check is still worth a hefty $1 million. It sounds like the check is the easy option, right? Well, how about we compare them both on day thirty-one? The check is still worth $1 million, while the penny now stands at $10,737,418.24! On the very last day, how did the single penny grow 10x the value of the $1 million-dollar check? It had a seemingly small goal to double every day for a full month. And neither you nor the penny could see the magic happening until the very last day. Just like the penny, you will not start to see the grand results of your small labors on day one, but on the day that those results present themselves, you will understand how and why.

4.   A Prime Example

To summarize the contents of Head on Fire, we found it beneficial to include an extremely relevant personal example. Writing a book takes a great deal of time and energy. People include writing a book on their lifetime bucket list, knowing the difficulty that comes with it. It takes more than a thought or an idea; it takes action. We believe in action, and we encourage you to take action on all of these important concepts and applications mentioned throughout the book. Easier said than done! As friends who both shared the same bucket list goal of writing a book, we also shared the same motivation for writing a book. That motivation was the biggest reason we were able to start and finish such a feat, all while balancing other important work and relationships.

Our motivation in writing this book hits a lot of key points that we discussed above. The first is that we did not write this for our own personal gain but rather in the interest of others. We were motivated to write this book because we shared a vision. This vision is to encourage as many people as we can to become the best version of themselves by putting their skillset to great use in the relentless pursuit of maximizing their potential. We realize that perfection is unachievable, but excellence is well within reach with the right mindset and action. Our motivation is to encourage others to replace laziness and gluttony with passion and purpose. Life is too short to waste it, especially knowing that everyone in the world has a particularly unique skill set that should be put to use. It would be a disservice to live a life without striving for excellence to improve the overall standard of humanity. We can all agree that nothing and no person is perfect, so it sounds to us like there are always improvements to be made. Make those improvements every day and encourage others to do so, and the result will be incredible. We want you to be the best person you can be by putting together your unique collection of skills to follow your passions and add value to the world as a whole.

We understand that our ideal example given above is a lot to digest. We included this example to show our best experience with a sturdy motive. This sturdy motive is well-intentioned, will stand true as time passes and life changes, and is pursued for the benefit of something much greater than the individual.

Before we put pen to paper, we not only took great inventory of ourselves individually but also as a team; we clearly defined something that was already within us. Sometimes, the answers to the hardest and most important questions to life are actually right inside you. For instance, you know what you enjoy doing, and you know why you enjoy doing it! You know what you're good at, and you now know what motivates you! It takes determination to find those answers, and it also takes real discipline to stay committed and motivated along your journey. We had to stay motivated throughout the entire process of writing this book, and it took maximum effort!

The definite overall goal was to create a book for the purpose of encouraging others to realize and maximize their potential. To obtain this goal, we had to first recognize the desire. Next, we created smaller goals in alignment with our chief aim or objective. These smaller goals included writing 500 words daily and completing certain chapters within a specific time frame. If you have a definite end goal while reading this book, you are well on your way. If you do not have a chief goal, keep an open mind, and continue to explore your interests. In the meantime, try to determine a smaller goal that may just lead you in the right direction to discover your "why." Having some sort of direction or vision is huge in realizing and maximizing your individual purpose.

Look below for a succinct example of how the contents of this chapter are specifically defined in the ongoing analogy for this guide to realize and maximize your potential:

1. Fuel = Passion to encourage others to be their best self

2. Vehicle = Becoming authors to write a book on what we are passionate about

3. Roadmap = Setting goals and checkpoints for when and how we want to complete this book

IV. Head on Fire

V. MARATHON

Would you rather have a penny today doubled every day for a full month or a check in your name for $1 million given to you today? By now, you are knowledgeable enough to choose the penny. You understand the power of compounding effort and the impact it can have on your journey. But all of this talk about creating strength and being the best version of yourself means nothing unless you're enjoying the fruits of your labor. Here, we want to focus on the importance of exercising the principles you have learned, day in and day out, but also taking each day to be present. It's not just about creating the dream but living it too.

Investing in the future does not have to mean sacrificing the present. The goal is not to finally have all of your ducks in a row by the time you die but rather to love the beauty in the struggle and celebrate each mile as you pass it and move onto the next. After all, life is a marathon, not a sprint.

1. **Not a Sprint**

Let's make this simple. Try working as hard as you can, as fast as you can, on achieving all your dreams at once. Some people will make it a few hours, others a couple of days, and a rare few even further, until realizing it cannot be done that quickly. If you are questioning this logic, we suggest you go back to the Head on Fire chapter and discover sturdier motives. These passions and motives are found within; hence, the use of the word discover. If you can achieve your greatest goal in one sitting, then you are limiting your options. Discovery raises you from settling for disappointing choices A or B to exploring options C and D, and finally, choosing a worthy option E.

With this understanding of real achievement being earned with the passage of time and investment, we can conclude that longevity is a huge factor. Victory is not owned, it is leased, and rent is due every day. Take a new car purchase, for example. It is true that you can make a hefty down payment to reduce the cost of future payments, but if you can cover the total cost of the car in one swoop, then the car is likely invaluable in comparison to your worth. When you discover a new desire or goal, use that energy and motivation to cut into the work early, but remember that the real valuable achievements come from the cost of paying dues gradually.

Limon

I had the pleasure of sitting down with Sarah Cohen, President and Founder of Route 11 Potato Chips. The chip company makes high-quality, home-grown potato chips. Cohen states, "Our focus, from day one, was to make a potato chip that's just better than the rest." They have done that and more, with their product being distributed nationwide, and media spots in both Oprah Winfrey's "O Magazine" and "The Today Show." From our discussion, if I had to choose one trait that set her apart from the rest, it was her care. She cares about the big picture! Hear her stance on quality: "Quality is not just reserved for a potato chip or a bag of potato chips or even an entire truckload of potato chips. We believe we are accountable for ensuring quality in every aspect of our existence as a company."

One of Route 11's earliest challenges involved equipment. Cohen was so focused on growing sales that there was little focus on properly maintaining the equipment. This lack of attention resulted in chronic breakdowns and interruptions in what was supposed to be a smooth flow of production. It also killed the bottom line and negated the whole purpose of being in business. The Route 11 Chip team discovered that the company was in much better shape when machinery was assessed daily. It allowed the company to be in a proactive position rather than reactively dealing with equipment breakdowns. Her business, which has grown into a nationally recognized brand, was her passion turned purpose. And what I took from this conversation was priceless.

Life should be treated the same, with care and frequent maintenance. Sarah Cohen found out early that the life of her business was far from a sprint but a marathon of trial and error. She understood that balance was key and that if you find balance in life, you will move swiftly towards your overall destination. We are rooting for her continued success, and we thank her for her time. Cohen made a point to mention this in her company's mission statement: "We strive to contribute to the quality of life of our families, friends and community because if we don't, what's the point?" We could not agree more.

1.1   Balancing Act

Gradual maintenance and balance are important not only for a company but for your own well-being. What makes a juggler so impressive? It is in their ability to simultaneously keep many objectives alive all at once for a long period of time. Life is a juggling act, and each pin is a priority. One pin does not take priority all of the time; rather, priorities shift as needed. The floor represents a harsh deadline. As a pin gets closer to the ground, a talented juggler knows to make this pin the priority before it falls to the floor. If a pin hits the floor, the task has failed. Failure is not permanent, but it is certainly better to keep everything up in the air than it is to recover one from the ground without dropping more pins. To fulfill our potential, we must be able to take on a lot of tasks simultaneously and tend to them as needed. Luke 12:48 states: "From everyone to whom much has been given, much will be required; and from the one to whom much has been entrusted, even more will be demanded." You will earn a portion of what you are willing to give. To achieve what you want to achieve, you must be able to handle the pressures required of such honors.

Authors of self-help books focus too much on the results. Not us; we encourage you to give your all in this present moment. We all want to be remembered, leave a legacy, and make a difference. But if you only focus on the result, you will dread the process. In reality, you are blessed to be alive and get to do all these things. You get to choose! Focus on loving the process. By allowing your fuel to fill you up, your work should excite and inspire you. There will be down days but keep perspective and realize that you are only better through these challenges. The result should be a byproduct of living the life you want to live. You should not live for the result; rather, live by greatness and allow the result, award, or achievement be a nice addition.

Living in the moment takes work; hence, why this tip we have for you is very tough to carry out in today's day and age. Put technology aside and simply be present. We have found that a big part of balance is to put our phones down, especially with others. When you sit down for a meal, today or tomorrow, get rid of the phone! Try being present with who you are breaking bread with or be present with yourself. The phone and other technology not only negatively affect our ability to think and focus, but it disconnects us from the current moment and the people that are in front of us. Ridding ourselves of distractions allows us to fill up with our fuel and our gratitude for it!

Do everything in moderation, from the small things to the big. Just as the juggler needs to shift priorities from pin to pin, you must also be fluid in your daily life. There are times when work or other obligations can be overwhelming, but nothing should be too overwhelming to where it rules your life for a great period of time. You need room to breathe, and you need the headspace to achieve. Moderation will prevent the inevitable burnout that comes with overworking. If the struggle you endure is greater than the fuel needed; you will burn out.

$$STRUGGLE > FUEL = BURNOUT$$

The fuel for your vehicle, the items you've identified early on in the book, has to be greater than your struggle. In order to maximize your potential, seek moderation in the important things. Here is a list of three pins with examples that are of the utmost importance to us. It's as follows:

1. Health
    a. Physical, Mental, Emotional, Spiritual

2. Relationships
    a. Family, Friends, Partners

3. Career
    a. Occupation, Finances, Education

These points all require focus and attention daily. But we have found that a healthy balance of all three automatically enhances the wellbeing of each individual item. Think of your life as healthy eating. Ideally, you want a balance of healthy fats and sugars found in vegetables and fruits. You also want hearty protein sources along with fiber-enriched carbohydrates. Every now and then, however, you have your favorite cheat meal or drink. This is fine; we encourage that break! In life, you need those rewarding breaks but make them worthwhile and deserved. Frame your life into your own properly proportioned meal. Make sure your time is consumed with the right things, the areas in which drive you further down your respective road. Find a balance between them and make sure you are taking the proper maintenance required to prevent burnout.

1.2   Lesson of the Geese

Some prefer to take on the journey of life alone, and it has been done before. This walk of isolation, however, will prevent you from growing and learning from others. The best journeys are those long roads taken together with a team. A lesson can be taken from a simple group of birds that naturally, though not by chance, migrate together. By taking a deeper look into the nature of a flock of geese, there are many things one can notice, whether it be the 'V' formation, continual position changes, and the seemingly excessive honking.

One reason goose fly in a 'V' formation is that it is the most aerodynamically efficient method. If each individual goose was to fly alone, they would each have to bear the same air resistance during flight, causing them to tire quickly. By flying in a 'V,' the front goose cuts through the air making the next goose's flight less tiring, and the goose after that as well all the way to the end. In addition to the formation of flight, the geese also switch positions during a long migration. The leading bird will eventually get tired from bearing all of the air resistance and can eventually tire toward the back of the formation as a new leader takes the front. According to the Smithsonian National Air and Space Museum, these birds can increase their total distance traveled by 70% under these circumstances. If you compare a flock of geese to a team, family, or other support systems, then it is easy to see how working as a unit can improve your journey as well. When a member of the team hits an obstacle, such as the front geese getting tired, the rest of the team can pick up that slack and ensure that no one is left behind.

Excessive honking is another big lesson to be taken from the geese. A great team is always great at communicating. There are so many easily avoidable problems within relationships, companies, educational systems, and other organizations simply because of a lack of communication. If one goose is unaware of its responsibility within the team and is then unable to do its job, the integrity of the 'V' is lost, and the team suffers because of it. Communication allows for the sharing of ideas, opinions, and goals such that the team can take a unified approach and move forward quickly in the desired direction.

An accountable team is invaluable. Mutual support and beneficial relationships can make or break a mission. The best team does not only hold each other accountable but are also very diverse in their skillsets. A great team plays to each individual's strengths and then comes together as a whole, well-rounded team. Picture a five-pointed star where the tip of each point touches an encompassing circle. Each star represents an individual on a team, each point represents a strength, and the empty space where the circle and star do not overlap are blind spots or weaknesses. A great team has many different people with many different strengths so that as a whole, the team is well-rounded and has no weaknesses. See the figure below for a model of a well-rounded team.

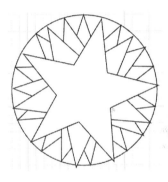

With mutual respect and love for one another, people can maximize both individual and group potential by focusing on their strengths and utilizing them for a greater cause.

2. Laying the Foundation

We split this book up into two sections as you know, realizing and maximizing. You've realized the potential, and now you're learning some of the essentials to maximize the journey. Although you are well past the realization portion, which is never really over remember; we do not want you to go full speed ahead...not yet. Although you are in the process of driving your vehicle, you understand the rules of the road and how to endure the journey; you can't go full speed until you have laid the proper foundation.

When construction workers build a skyscraper, they don't start building up immediately, no. Instead, they start by digging below the surface in order to create the proper foundation. Your journey is no different. If we want to build up, we must first dig below and develop the infrastructure needed to succeed. If you were to start building a skyscraper high with no foundation, eventually a slight gust of wind will knock the entire building over! Build your foundation first so that you can endure the trials and tribulations that will come with your success. Whether you are a high school or college graduate or transitioning from one area of work to another, you need to lay your foundation.

2.1 Apprenticeship

Leonardo da Vinci, arguably the most famous artist to ever exist, started out as an apprentice painter before ever touching a brush. He went on to paint the Mona Lisa. Observing the lives of past and present, "Masters," we can detect the phase in their lives where they took on the role of apprenticeship, also known as experiential learning. Although this phase of life never receives recognition for great achievement or discovery, the apprenticeship phases plant the seed for future success.

The great Benjamin Franklin didn't know what he wanted to do for a living. In the 18th century, this decision was up to his father. Luckily, his father realized young Franklin's potential. He knew what his passions were, reading and writing. Before long, Benjamin joined the printing business to be an apprentice to his brother James at the age of 12. Back then, apprenticeships were the approximate of an internship today. However, the contracts that apprentices were signed under were harsh. The agreement would require long work hours and years of commitment before leaving. Franklin was put to work, doing all kinds of tasks; nonetheless, he worked hard and learned very quickly. In 1721, his older brother James decided to start a controversial newspaper, the *New England Courant*. It was so controversial that in 1723, the Massachusetts legislature decided that the paper mocked religion and the government. They put James in jail and stated that he was no longer allowed to print the paper.

James figured out a way to publish the paper using Franklin's name. At the age of 17, Benjamin Franklin was the new publisher of the *Courant*. To legitimize the move, James relieved Franklin of his public apprenticeship agreement but not fully. While making it look like he was relieved of the agreement, he insisted on a secretive apprenticeship agreement that would ensure Franklin's commitment to the business. While Franklin enjoyed being the publisher, he enjoyed his freedom more. Taking advantage of the secret agreement, knowing that James would be in a sticky situation if it was known by the public, he left.

Franklin went on to open his own printing shop in Philadelphia. The shop printed Pennsylvania's currency, his own paper the *Pennsylvania Gazette* and his *Poor Richard's Almanac*. He was widely successful in these pursuits, and most of his wealth came from those two publications. During the revolution, he became the first United States Postmaster General. He became more active in national and international affairs and politics. Printer turned diplomat; Franklin became one of the most influential political writers, heroes, and innovators of all time. His life of legacy was not to be forgotten. As he is considered one of America's most influential Founding Fathers, he has been honored through and through. There is a reason Benjamin Franklin's head is displayed on the largest valued bill in U.S. circulation.

Benjamin Franklin notably had one of the greatest stories of following to leading. His initial act to follow opened larger doors, unimaginable to him at the time. Franklin was fortunate to have a father that understood this framework to learn and grow. The framework exposed him to the right and wrong ways to operate and the fundamentals of printing. This framework created a rapid learning sequence for Franklin, causing him to branch out on his own...to do it better.

Before you lead, you must follow. Upon seeing how things are done, experiment! Go to the beat of a different drum and try to enhance what was previously taught. Never be afraid to outshine the master because, "If your superior is a falling star, there is nothing to fear from outshining him" (Robert Greene, Power, 2000). Just as a parent's goal is to raise their children to be better than them, it will bring a mentor great pride to see you continue and better their work. Part of maximizing your individual potential is the capacity to stand tall under a skillful master who can provide extreme value to the future. If the future is not yet clear, foresee future events and possible outcomes. In other words, work smart. Funnel all the information that is presented to you and do your own analysis. Does it fit into your life? Does it align with your fuel and vehicle? You will learn if your passions are aligned with your work. You will learn whether it was right for you in the first place. Jumpstart your legacy by practicing patience and implementing this learning framework. Follow first, make sure to funnel information and sift through every bit, lead second.

2.2 Delayed Gratification

There are actions that we take in our lives that serve ourselves, and there are actions that we take that serve our senses. Serving yourself is acting in accordance with your fuel and your vehicle to achieve something that is in your own best interest and aligned with your values through immense effort, discipline, and time. Serving your senses is simply engaging in an activity for short-term stimulation. Delaying gratification is forgoing these simple pleasures in pursuit of achievement, relationship, or skill that will provide long-term satisfaction. Dr. Walter Mischel, a Stanford graduate in psychology, speaks to this saying, "Self-control is crucial for the successful pursuit of long-term goals. It is equally essential for developing the self-restraint and empathy needed to build caring and mutually supportive relationships." Everyone has these short-term temptations to indulge in a substance or activity, and sometimes, the consequences are not severe. We touched on moderation and how moderate consumption of simple, immediate pleasures will not have a lasting effect. Think about the previous sentence again. The consumption of simple immediate pleasures will not have a lasting effect. What is consumed will invoke an instant positive reaction that will not last. We challenge you to minimize these forms of instant gratification in pursuit of a lasting effect!

Here is a small example of instant gratification versus patient achievement that everyone can relate to: microwaveable vs. prepared meals. Microwaving food is quick, often flavorful, and satisfies hunger. The food may have a positive effect on the taste buds while meeting your temporary needs, but is it serving you in a great way? Prepared and balanced meals offer you the same instant reward of accomplishing in the kitchen and fulfilling short-term hunger, but there is more than that. This meal serves your body by enriching you with powerful nutrients that will energize you throughout the days to come. The better choice is obvious and highlights why it is important to allocate time to tasks that serve you and set you up in the future. Staying patient and disciplined will aid in your journey in all aspects. Let's loosen this microwave mentality as we aim to achieve long-term goals with greater and long-lasting payouts.

1. Faith > Fear

Along your journey to maximization, there is one force that can stop you dead in your tracks. That force is fear, a force so strong that it has the ability to drain us of our mental and psychic energy. We have all experienced fear in our lives, fear of the past, the present, and the future. Fear fills us up with uncertainty, stopping us from continuing further with whatever it may be, a relationship, a job, or an experience. What's causing this formidable force? Who's strong enough to create such destruction? It's you.

We know that you have caught a glimpse of fear in your life. We'd bet that the fear you've experienced is probably incomparable to the horror someone else has gone through. There are scary things in this world, unimaginable things that we cannot all comprehend. If you are like most people, you fear the shortness of life. But don't stop there because you are not like most people. Although this fear is recognized, we can draw two conclusions: time is finite, and it's our greatest asset. Every day, we grow older, and we come closer to death. That in itself should be motivation enough to move forward. It's hard to move when the destination is unclear. People fear that they are purposeless, that their road is leading to nowhere, fast. You'd think people would run from this fear, but the opposite is true. Instead of moving forward, people settle. Do not under any circumstances, settle! As you take on this marathon of maximizing your potential, we want to give you the key to combating this fear. Fortunately, fear is only a state of mind. Though hard to escape, this state of mind can be combated by an even stronger force. If you find yourself taking these leaps of fear along your road, we ask you to jump with us and take the leap of faith.

There are those individuals who seem to find purpose early. They seem destined to become a doctor or a professional athlete as if they were born with natural talent and a perfectly drawn out path. This happens rarely, but that does not mean that the potential and direction do not lie within the next person. And most of the time, the purpose appears at the right time, in the right moment as long as you are taking your steps forward. Naturally, people hope for their moment of clarity and realization of what is in store but hoping for an outcome will do nothing.

Instead of having hope, have faith. What is the difference between hope and faith? American actor and comedian, Jim Carrey, stated in a speech to a graduating class, "I don't believe in hope. Hope is a beggar. Hope walks through the fire. Faith leaps over it." Having hope is easy; it's wishing. Faith, unlike hope, is an understanding and knowing that everything will have a resolution. Knowing that something is going to happen, even when the odds aren't in your favor, is an act of faith. Faith is a call to action.

World-changers, people who do the unthinkable often use faith as the basis for all decision-making. Martin Luther King campaigned against the segregation of Blacks in the Southern United States. King did this in a time of extreme violence and hatred toward the Black people of the 1950s and 60s. King was inspired by his religion, Christianity, and the peaceful teachings of Mahatma Gandhi. King, bearer of a Nobel Peace Prize, is the most well-known spokesperson and leader in the Civil Rights Movement. His life-impacting thoughts were manifested through faith in his life. No matter if faith is instilled within a person through the practice of religion, it will always have an impact on the journey to achieve the dreams that lie within.

Limon

Personally, faith was a self-embarked journey. Despite going to a Catholic school up until the sixth grade, faith did not play a big part in my life. At the age of twelve, seeing my grandmother battle through cancer, I reflected back to the basic prayers I had learned in Elementary school. It became comforting to pray each day, hoping for resolve. To my surprise, the prayers were being answered over and over again. I carried hope and worry before, but it was not until this liberating moment that I understood the strength of faith. Faith is now not only practice, but a way of life for me.

God may be the answer for us, but that does not mean it is the answer for you. Whatever form of grace you identify with, God or maybe the Universe, have faith. Find your shield, something greater than yourself in which you trust and believe.

All of the life-altering characteristics presented in this book will be tested, and faith is no exception. Failure is the truest test of one's faith. When things don't go according to plan, faith is easily lost. Not only is faith lost in the person, but it's also lost in all future outcomes. Hope is more mental than anything. Faith, at its core, involves heart and spirit. It cannot be explained logically nor understood through a single dimension. In tough times, the mind can become weak and play tricks. The heart and spirit are where one must look when they need deeper answers. Many do not believe what they cannot see. Little do they know that with faith, the path will illuminate in times of darkness and doubt. This strength, faith, is not just a notion people cling to in troubled times but an essential part of living.

The person you are becoming right now needs faith and spirituality. Faith is a binding characteristic of all learnt materials in the realization section and this section on maximization. What happens when an objective or goal is not met? What if a long sought-after plan doesn't fall through? What happens when roadblocks are erected? Faith is what ties loose ends and bursts through the barriers that stand in the way. Fear, the devil's trick, will steer people away from their goals. The only way to combat fear is with faith. Ralph Waldo Emerson once wrote, "Do the thing you fear, and the death of fear is certain." If fears are confronted, faith is the reason.

Like the air that is breathed, oxygen nourishes the mind, while faith nourishes the heart. If one truly wants to find purpose early, faith is a strength that must be practiced. There comes a point when the practice of faith becomes a lifestyle. Some people are influenced by family members, religious communities, and acquaintances; others have no influence. Let this chapter be a starting point for a self-embarked journey of ultimate growth. Eliminate hope and, instead, adopt faith, go with courage because "Hope walks through fire, faith leaps over it."

Action Steps: Faith

1. Confront your fears - Use faith as your shield

2. Have faith - Believe in others, your purpose, and most importantly, yourself.

3. Eliminate hope - Wishing isn't enough

2. Disclaimer: Success is yours to define

Transcend's aim is not to define success for you. We will let other authors claim that they know what success is for their readers but not us. We want you to define your own success. We do believe that success is found in the happiness you experience along your journey, but it's all up to you. Assuming you have the proper fuel and vehicle, all of which you have defined; it will lead to a happy journey! By using this book as your toolkit, you are eliminating the chance of ever feeling remorse for choosing this path.

V. Marathon
1. Not a Sprint
   1.1 Balancing Act
   1.2 Lessons of the Geese
2. Laying the Foundation
   2.1 Apprenticeship
   2.2 Delayed Gratification
3. Faith > Fear
4. Note on Success

VI. DESTINATION

1. Humble and Kind

Country artist Tim McGraw, wrote a song entitled,
"Humble and Kind." This song is a healthy reminder
of teachings we often forget. Some of the simple lines
sung by artists of all genres provide the greatest
perspective. Not only does this song mention reasons
for not holding grudges or wasting time; it mentions
your journey. When you get to where you've been
going, don't forget to turn back around and help the
next one in line. Once your cup is full, allow it to
overflow onto others. We know you will reach your
destination and are excited for you! And we are
excited about the impact you will have on all the lives
you end up touching. Hopefully, this final chapter will
be the one that sticks with you the most. At the end
of the day, people are the most important, and that's
what this chapter is about.

1.1 People Focus

The average salary in the United States is roughly $55,000; the cost for a company to maintain those employees is 1.4 times more, costing $77,000. On top of a base salary and substantial bonuses, in some cases, companies offer the following: life insurance, health coverage, dental plans, pension plans, stock options, 401(k), tuition, and much, much more. This doesn't include the costs companies incur for an employee to sit in their building on a square footage basis. Some of the biggest and boldest companies today provide their employees with daily lunch, season tickets to their favorite sports team, and even the ability to bring their furry friends to the office.

We want to highlight the importance that companies place on people. The top organizations in the world invest heavily into theirs, and it's crucial that you invest in yours too. Throughout your life, think of all the people you have come across and count each one; you most likely can't count that high. You have met people from all around the world and shaken the hands of those on different journeys, but what have you given them? We aren't asking you to give up life savings, but can you give them your full attention? Can you give them a smile? That's all we're asking for.

Whether you want to organize an activist group to solve a problem you feel passionate about, raise capital for your dream company, or simply organize a pick-up basketball game, you will need great relationships. The relationships we have with our coworkers, communities, and even our adversaries are means of achieving goals. And nurturing these relationships help the other parties to achieve their own goals as well; this is what it is all about. We can guess that if you made it this far into our book, you care deeply about leaving an impact on this planet. You care deeply about people, even if you sometimes neglect these urges; you care. It's not only okay to care; it's important to care...it's part of our nature as humans. Country singer and songwriter, Luke Bryan, has a song titled "Most People are Good." We sing in unison with Luke, as we believe most people are good, and everyone has stored potential just waiting to be maximized to the fullest. You can start them on that journey, just as someone ignited the fire to start yours.

The Law of Reciprocity reaffirms our belief. Have you noticed that when you smile at someone, they smile back? It is considered the most powerful law of human nature, where if you are to act positively towards someone, they will respond positively in return. Kindness is most often returned with more kindness. This is a positive loop that should be taken advantage of, not only for your own benefit but for the benefit of all. The Golden Rule as stated in the Bible is "Do unto others as you would have them do unto you." This rule is sprinkled throughout many religions, such as Hinduism where Karma is their take on how beings in the universe should interact. The Law of Reciprocity is calling on all people to spread kindness and make our world a better place. It's a chance to highlight the good in the world for everyone to see.

Do you question the times you were done wrongly? There was a man who saw a snake being burned to death and decided to take it out of the fire.

While doing so, the snake bit him. The bite caused the man to drop the snake back into the burning flames. The man then tried pulling the snake back out, and the snake bit him again. An onlooker asked the man, "Sir, why do you keep helping the snake live if it continues to bite?" The man replied, "The nature of the snake is to bite, but that's not going to change my nature, which is to help." With the assistance of a metal rod, the man saved the snake from burning to death.

Do not change your nature simply because someone harms you or is unfair. It's not your reputation that matters but your character and conscience. Having a strong character that focuses on people creates the strongest leaders and the strongest believers. Believe that the Law of Reciprocity can take you and others to new heights. As leaders, it's our job to care deeply about the goals of others as well. It is our caring for others that motivates us to work as hard as we do. Focus on people, focus on kindness.

1.2 Our Guiding Light

Your parents, siblings, grandparents, spouse and friends are counting on you. We often chat about what light guides us along our path, and the answer continues to be our loved ones. Our final words before each day are said in prayer, asking God for three things: health, happiness, and safety for those around us. It's those three things for our family and friends that we hold fixed in our minds as we push ourselves to overcome obstacles and take on daunting challenges.

Through every sunny or cloudy day, our parents, in particular, have been our beacon of light. Our parents have been the lighthouse on the shore, guiding us home no matter the condition of the weather. They have never given up on us and have always given their unconditional love, and we are extremely grateful for them. We urge you to look at your own life; who is your lighthouse? Who hasn't given up on you and continues to be there for you, no matter what storm you are going or have gone through? No matter what cards you were dealt in life; there are people that love you.

Dearest friends can also serve this purpose, and there are no limits to love and support. It is important to know who loves you unconditionally and to embrace it. There is a quote for such a friend in Proverbs 18:24 that states, "He who has unreliable friends soon comes to ruin, but there is a friend who sticks closer than a brother." Be grateful for such reliable friends and strive to be that ideal friend for them because they deserve that same unconditional love that may guide them along their journey.

As we all have one life, your family members and friends are choosing to spend their limited time with you. In a world where things are more fabricated than ever, they choose to believe in you! These relationships serve a significant purpose, to empower and awaken the greatness that lies inside of you. Strengthen these bonds, nurture them, and watch as the power of mutual connection overcomes any obstacle and acts as that light peeking through, no matter how gloomy the horizon. Your journey is much easier when you have the support of your loved ones, and you are able to help them succeed in their own undertakings.

We should all strive for leadership at any age where there is even the possibility of positive influence, such as helping a friend study for a test and encouraging them of great performance. But where you will have substantial influence is parenthood. It's guaranteed that when one has a child of their own, that child will look towards their parents as a model for who they should be. Children are sponges absorbing everything around them, good and bad. They are the purest of slates, awaiting to be led in a direction. It's miraculous that humans can make another person. We can be the master coordinator and design of the most complex system in existence; leaders of the future generations. Parenthood is a chance to have the most substantial impact ever. It is continually said by parents far and wide that the moment they held their child for the first time was the greatest moment of their entire lives. As distant as that might be for us now, we understand the importance of being a parent and are grateful for all the parents out there, raising our future generation.

We are grateful for all of the partners and lovers in the world. Romantic, intimate love is exciting and most importantly, beautiful. As children are born into this world, it's important to fill them with love because that love will be outwardly given back to people or groups of people. We can share our love infinitely with friends, a stranger, and with those who need it. It's always there, and it never leaves. The love you share with your partner, husband or wife should always bring you home, to a place of internal peace, happiness, and fulfillment. We promise to be the best husbands and fathers we can be, as we understand the importance of both.

1.3 Our Promise

American philosopher, author, and public speaker, Wayne Dyer once said, "If you change the way you look at things, the things you look at change." Treat someone for who they are, and they become worse. On the contrary, if you treat someone where they could be, they will end up exactly where they should be.

Everybody enters this world with a clean slate although filled with varying dreams, energy levels, and ambitions. We all start from a place of inexperience and vulnerability. From the outside, you are only what you are and have experienced. After all, "The expert at something was once a beginner." A key difference driving you from beginner to expert is optimistic belief; the belief that life can be more, you can become more, and that you have much to give. Treating someone as they are is placing a restriction on their potential, and while this is still a belief, it's a limiting one. Treating someone for what they can be empowers them to become that which they wish to be. Quitting is the cessation of belief in someone or something when there is progress to be made. With empowering belief, every day, students begin to learn and grow and become valuable members of the world. Choose to believe and act on those beliefs as you transform formidable will into experience, knowledge, and reality.

Those who turn those empowering beliefs into reality are often seen as anomalies, as unrealistic. These people did not start off where they are now. Beyoncé Knowles says in Eminem's song *Walk on Water*, "Cause I'm only human, just like you." This song should speak to everybody showing that celebrities and wide influencers are just people too. People who saw the potential inside themselves, or someone else saw it in them and transformed it into action until they achieved their goals, thus earning this idealistic status. You have what it takes!

It would be ignorant of us to claim that we know where you will end up at the beginning or end of your journey. But we know that there is no physical destination or end. Your true destination is a peak mental state of improvement. You are responsible for the exploration and pursuit of this self-improvement. We can guarantee that the only method of reaching the potential inside of you is to start today and relentlessly pursue excellence. Humans only ever use a very small portion of the potential that is inside of them. What's limiting that stored potential? The answer to that question could be answered with an excuse, such as being "too old" or "not having time." It could also be answered legitimately, as it can be hard to unlock. Where are the answers as to how? Remember, age is just a validation of existence, and every person on this planet has the same twenty-four hours in a day. With this being said, go achieve and become the best version of yourself for "You cannot pour from an empty cup." You must take action to fill your cup, whether through education or experiences. Once your cup is filled, then your cup can overflow and begin to help others.

The Earth, so small in comparison to the universe, is home to the only life we know. It is home to more than 7.7 billion people, the aggregate of all joys and all sufferings. It's home to all the dreams fulfilled and unfulfilled. Do you find yourself picturing a different life? Or maybe you are satisfied where you are but know you can do more? Many are discouraged by the belief that their actions will make no difference here on earth. It's hard to conceptualize the magnitude of our actions, let alone 7.7 billion people. It is rational to question with such a large population size: what is the significance of just one life? Will the way I spend my mornings and afternoons matter?

A person, no matter the sphere of influence, has a great impact. Everything you do will affect the people around you, whether you intend to or not, and the earlier you start, the more profound your impact. Those around you will then feed off your pursuit, creating a standard to meet. Many are paralyzed by the magnitude of the universe, and their minds can trick them into taking the easiest road but raise the standard! What we ask is that you realize that at the end of the day, being the best version of yourself isn't really about you. If it were all about you, these negative beliefs might be right, and you would likely tire or give up. But the truth is, being the best version of yourself raises the average and has a cascading effect on those around you who are then inspired to raise their own bar. Striving to realize and maximize your potential is the way to join the whole in pursuit of moving humanity forward. Every day, you get to decide the effort you give. You get to decide to choose faith and love as a backbone for good.

Choose to raise the standard because it matters that much. We will quantify it for you:

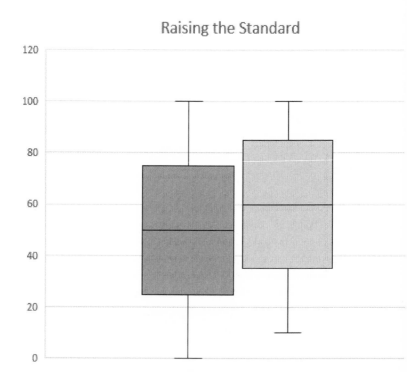

Raising the Standard

The graph above represents the distribution of percent effort given by the entire population. The plot on the left shows the current standard, and the plot on the right shows an increased standard after the majority of people give 10% more. This example can allow you to visualize what is deemed average with respect to the whole (solid black horizontal line) and how everyone's empowerment to give 10% more will raise this standard.

Effort is difficult to measure; here is another example in the form of time: if you work from 9:00 am to 5:00 pm every day, giving 1% more would equate to just 5 minutes. You are doing your part if your pursuit of greater good is an extra 5 minutes per day. You will succeed as a result and achieve everything you ever wanted. We are thankful that you have chosen a mission that serves others and contributes to something bigger than yourself. We used to lay on the asphalt driveway staring up at the stars and moon, asking ourselves, "what is this all about?" The answer stretches further than us. We'll repeat, striving to realize and maximize your potential is the way to join the whole in pursuit of moving humanity forward.

The world is an orchestra, playing one grand song in unison. Each of us belongs to a section with an instrument to play, and it's our job to play our instrument to the best of our ability for this song to sound its best and for it to call on others to play. Our final promise is to realize and maximize our potential, and the universe is counting on you to do the same.

ABOUT THE AUTHORS

Forrest Limon

Receiving his Bachelor of Science (B.S.) in Finance, Forrest has been asked to join JPMorgan Chase full-time in New York City starting 2020. Studying at Mercy College and the London School of Economics, he has gained a keen interest in capital markets and investment strategy. As part of the Business Honors Program, Forrest has interned with multiple Fortune 500 companies. He loves spending time with his closest family members and friends, outdoors preferably. Through a mixture of deeply rooted values and diverse experience, Forrest is chasing towards a deeper understanding of others to one day assume a leadership role.

Nathan Wagner

Nathan is an Aerospace Engineering and Physics double major. He is a leader, learner, and focused problem-solver determined to propel the STEM industry forward through the application of fundamental understanding, technical knowledge, and economic considerations. Before becoming an author, Nathan has pursued the goal of motivating and inspiring others through leading a Self-Improvement Seminar and Mentoring for the CEED Galileo Engineering Community. His character and achievements have been recognized on multiple occasions through merit scholarships such as Pamplin Scholar and Leader tuition awards. He believes in living a life full of passion and purpose and encourages others to do the same

To hear more about the Authors and this read visit: limonwagner.com

Made in the
USA
Columbia, SC